This Book is easy enough for the "First Time Repairer", yet detailed enough to teach the most experienced Technician...

THE LAPTOPS EXTERIOR

The Laptops Exterior; the Keyboard:

pg 17-**Replacing a missing key:**

pg 17-**Repairing a Key**

pg18-**How the keyboard connects to the motherboard**

The Laptops Exterior; the Touchpad:

pg 18-**Repairing broken buttons**

pg 19-**Replacing or Repairing the Touchpad**

pg19-**Using the built in features on the Touchpad**

The Laptops Exterior; the Ports, Input and Output Connections on a Laptop:

pg 20-**VGA/Serial Port/DVI**

pg 20-**HDMI**

pg 20-**FireWire**

pg 20-**S-Video**

pg 21-**Printer Port - parallel port**

pg 21-**Docking Station Port**

pg 21-**USB**

pg 21-**Audio Out/Headphone Jack Port**

pg 22-**PC Card Slot, Remote Control Slot, SD Slot**

pg 22-**Ethernet/Modem Port**

The Laptops Exterior: The Palmrest:

pg 22-**Repairing broken screw posts**

pg 23-**Replacing the Palmrest**

pg 23-**Buttons or Switches on the Palmrest**

The Laptops Exterior: The Screen:

pg 23-**The Layers of a laptops screen and their purposes**

pg 24-**How the screen works**

pg 24-**LED vs. LCD (ccfl)**

pg 25-**Signs of a cracked screen, what to look for**

pg 25-**Determining Failure to the screens circuit panel board**

pg 25-**Replacing the screen**

pg 26-**Tablet PC Screens**

pg 27-**The digitizer panel, its uses and how to replace**

The Laptops Exterior: The Bottom Base – Housing:

pg 27-**Repairing broken or missing screw posts**

pg 27-**Removing the bottom base from the motherboard**

pg 27-**Replacing the bottom base**

The Laptops Exterior: The Access Areas on the Underside of a Laptop:

pg 28-**Hard Drive Cover**

pg 28-**RAM Cover**

pg 28-**Wi-Fi Cover**

pg 28-**Optical Drive Plate/Cover**

pg 29-**CPU/Heatsink Cover**

The Laptops Exterior: The Access Areas on the Underside of a Laptop:

pg 29-**Hard Drive, Battery and Power on/off lights and their locations**

pg 29-**The Laptops Battery and All About it**

pg 30-**The Media Strip Lights and Icons**

pg 30-**Using Different Colors for the LED Lights and Why**

Laptop Power Sources and Management

Laptop Power Sources and Management; The AC Adapter (charging cord):

pg 31-The AC cord end, the DC cord end and the power inverter box

pg 31-Testing the AC Adapter

pg 32-Repairing the Cord

pg 32-Repairing the Plug Tip

Laptop Power Sources and Power Management; The Battery:

pg 33-Proper Usage Tips

pg 34-Determining Failure and Drainage of the Battery

pg 34-Replacing the Battery

Laptop Power Sources and Power Management; Managing the Power Settings in Windows:

pg 35-Navigating to the Power Settings in Windows

pg 35-Optimizing the Power Settings

pg 36-Preinstalled Power Management Software and Drivers

Laptop Power Sources and Power Management; Power Options in BIOS Setup:

pg 36-Configuring and Location

Laptop RAM or Memory Types

Laptop RAM (random access memory) or Memory Types; DDR 1-DDR 2-DDR 3, microDimm:

pg 36-The most commonly used Memory

Laptop RAM (random access memory) or Memory Types; Types of RAM, Pin Counts and speeds:

pg 36-Dedicated RAM, Integrated RAM

pg 37-Slot Loaded RAM, the types, and how to insert or remove the sticks

Laptop RAM (random access memory) or Memory Types; Using only one slot, is it ok?

pg 37-Using only one of the two (or more) slots available

pg 37-Upgrading RAM

Laptop Hard Drive Types and Compatibility (the 3 main types)

Laptop Hard Drive Types and Compatibility; Sata:

pg 37-**Serial ATA, Hard drive Specifications, Upgrading, Speeds**

Laptop Hard Drive Types and Compatibility; Pata-IDE

pg 38-**Parallel ATA, Hard Drive Specs, upgrading, speeds**

Laptop Hard Drive Types and Compatibility; SSD

pg 38-**Solid State Drive, Drive specifications, upgrading and speeds**

Laptop Cooling

Laptop Cooling; Fan and Heatsink functions and types:

pg 38-**The Heat sink Pipes and Radiator**

pg 39-**The reason for a heat sink and fan**

pg 39-**What components are the heat sinks cooling plates covering?**

pg 39-**Fan-less Cooling Design**

Laptop Cooling; External/Internal cooling options:

pg 39-**USB exhaust port fan**

pg 40-**Cooling pad, to use or not to use**

pg 40-**Thermal paste usage and application**

pg 41-**Using copper shims on the heatsink**

Laptop Cooling; CPU Fan Modification:

pg 41-**How to make the fan run full speed all the time**

pg 42-**Fixing fan noise issues**

Laptop Upgrading

Laptop Upgrading; Laptop Wireless Options (configuration and install):

pg 43-**How to install wireless if none exists**

pg 43-**Adding internal antennas for Wi-Fi signal**

pg 43-Wireless card types, location of card port

The Laptops Internal Parts and Components

The Laptops Internal Parts and Components; the Motherboard:

pg 43-Differences between a Desktop PC motherboard and a Laptop motherboard

pg 44-Colors of Motherboards, Icons on the motherboard, Part Identification

pg 44-Attached mini boards, daughter boards

pg 44-Ability to use a compatible motherboard if an exact replacement is not available...

The Laptops Internal Parts and Components; DC Jack:

pg 45-Plugging In, Preventing damage to the DC Jack and to the Adapter plug

pg 45-Purpose of the DC Jack

pg 45-Pin connection vs. Wire and Plug connection

pg 45-The process of replacing the DC Jack

The Laptops Internal Parts and Components; CD/DVD/Blu-ray Drives:

pg 46-Proper cleaning of the Optical Lens

pg 46-Slot loaded vs. Slide tray loading discs and drives

The Laptops Internal Parts and Components; Floppy Drives:

pg 47-External floppy drives, internal drives and their use today

The Laptops Internal Parts and Components; SD Card / Slot Cards:

pg 47-Usages and location on the laptop

pg 47-Different types of SD and Slot Loading Cards and Peripherals

pg 48-Setting up Ready-Boost on the SD card

Laptop Issues

Laptop Issues; Non-Powering On Issues:

pg 48-Process of elimination testing procedures

pg 48-Determining the cause (software or hardware related)

Laptop Issues; Overheating Issues:

pg 51-Random shut downs and the reason why

pg 52-The importance of a proper cleaning on a regular basis

pg 52-Fixing overheating issues and different methods used

Laptop Issues; Non Booting Issues:

pg 52-Determining the cause, process of elimination testing

pg 54-Laptop Powering On But Has Blank-Black Screen

pg 55-Laptop Powers On, Then Immediately Shuts Down

Laptop Issues; CD-DVD Drive not working / not recognized:

pg 55-Deleting the upper and lower filters from the registry

Laptop Screen / Video Issues

Laptop Screen / Video Issues; No video on the laptops screen:

pg 56-Connecting an external screen or monitor for testing purposes

pg 56-Determining if it is a video issue or if it is screen problems

Laptop Screen / Video Issues; Lines on the screen:

pg 56-Start by checking the display cable, here's how…

pg 56-Determining if there is damage to the screens rear circuit board panel

pg 57-Temporary repair to remedy the line issue

Laptop Screen / Video Issues; Faint image but no backlight:

pg 57-Process of elimination testing to determine the fault

Power Issues

Power Issues; No Power at All:

pg 59-Troubleshooting and process of elimination testing procedure

pg 59-Continuity or short circuit test

pg 60-Resistance and Resistors

pg 60-**Types of Resistors**

pg 60-**Measuring a fuse on board with a digital or analog multimeter**

pg 60-**Testing Coil/Inductors**

pg 61-**Testing Diodes**

pg 61-**Testing electrolytic capacitor with digital capacitance meter**

pg 61-**ESR Meter Testing**

pg 61-**Testing Ceramic Capacitors**

pg 61-**Testing Voltage Regulator IC**

pg 62-**Transistor Failure**

pg 62-**Testing Field Effect Transistor (FET or Mosfet)**

Wireless Issues

Wireless Issues; Local Access Only Issues:

pg 63-**Resetting the router**

pg 63-**Troubleshooting the issue, determining if the issue is software or virus related**

Hard Drive Issues

Hard Drive Issues; Failing hard drives, pinpointing the issue:

pg 64-**Listening for issues, Clicking and grinding noise**

Repairing the Laptop Screen

Repairing the Laptop Screen; Front Bezel Replacing:

pg 64-**Removing the front bezel without breaking it**

pg 65-**Replacing a broken front bezel, choosing webcam capability for the bezel**

pg 65-**Fixing hinge lid locks that are located on the front bezel**

Repairing the Laptop Screen; LCD bulb repair and replacement:

pg 65-**The LCD bulb plastic and aluminum housing and its importance**

Repairing the Laptop Screen; LED light strip repair and replacement:

pg 65-This is the new "common" light source being used, here's why…

pg 66-How to repair or Replace the LED light strip

pg 66-Do LED screens use a power inverter? Here's your answer…

Repairing the Laptop Screen; Power Inverter repair and replacement:

pg 66-Determining if the inverter board is good or bad

pg 66-Obtaining a replacement inverter

Motherboard Repair Instructions

Motherboard Repair Instructions; Tools used to test the board:

pg 67-To use an anti-static wristband, or not?

Motherboard Repair Instructions; Troubleshooting the Motherboard:

pg 67-MEASURING:

Motherboard Repair Instructions; How and What to Test, Where to start:

pg 69-The Process of elimination testing

Motherboard Repair Instructions; The Components on the motherboard:

pg 74-LAPTOP COMPONENTS

Motherboard Repair Instructions; PCB (printed circuit board) Repair Methods:

pg 79-Repairing damaged traces on the motherboard

pg 79-Repairing damaged pin contacts, eye rings, C-Ring repair techniques

pg 80-Re-insulating the motherboard (the green or blue color Overcoat sealant)

pg 80-Replacing a damaged component

pg 81-Board-Flex repair and prevention

Hard Drive Repairing

Hard Drive Repairing; Disassembling the Hard Drive:

pg 82-Removing the screws to replace the circuit board card

pg 82-**Removing the screws to disassemble the cover to gain access to the inner components**

<u>Hard Drive Repairing;</u>   What to look for inside the hard drive:

pg 82-**The parts that make up a hard drive, the location and their uses**

<u>Hard Drive Repairing;</u>   Repairing Hard Drive Failure Issues:

pg 83-**Transfer of the disc/data platters**

Speaker and Audio Issues

<u>Speaker and Audio Issues;</u>   No sound from speakers or from headphone jack:

pg 83-**The first thing to do is to reinstall the most current driver software update**

pg 83-**Visual inspection of the motherboard, speaker and port connections**

<u>Speaker and Audio Issues;</u>   Replacing the Speakers:

pg 84-**Unplugging the speakers, cleaning the speakers**

pg 84-**Determining speaker failure issues**

pg 84-**How to replace blown speakers**

<u>Hard Drive Repairing;</u>   Determining failure of the controller chip on the motherboard:

pg 85-**Process of elimination testing conclusion**

Removable Media

<u>Removable Media;</u>   SD Cards, SSD, USB Devices, Flash Drives, Thumb Drives, External Hard Drives:

pg 85-**Description of the most common types of removable media**

Laptop Add On Components

<u>Laptop Add On Components;</u>   Cooling Pads, Plug In USB Devices, Accessories:

pg 86-**Some common add on components**

Liquid Spills to the Laptop

<u>Liquid Spills to the Laptop;</u>   Steps to take to prevent future damage:

pg 86-**How To Repair a Laptop/Notebook That Has Had Liquid Spilled On It**

pg 86-**THE FIRST THING TO DO WHEN LIQUID HAS SPILLED ONTO/INTO LAPTOP** pg 88-**Removing the Battery, the AC Adapter and why**

pg 88-**Keyboard Covers**

Liquid Spills to the Laptop; Cleaning the Remaining Liquid:

pg 88-**Materials and cleaning solutions used to remove the liquid spill residue**

pg 88-**Knowing what spilled by its appearance**

pg 89-**Cleaning the keyboard**

Liquid Spills to the Laptop; What happens if left unattended:

pg 89-**Component corrosion sets in**

pg 89-**The damage it causes and prolonged damage common to a liquid spill**

Liquid Spills to the Laptop; Repairing any damage caused by the spill:

pg 90-**Proper way to remove the corrosion that resides on the components after a spill**

pg 90-**Testing and replacing damaged components**

pg 90-**Baking the motherboard to dissipate the residual liquid under IC chips**

A Laptops Southbridge, Northbridge and GPU/CPU Chipsets

A laptops Southbridge, Northbridge and GPU/CPU Chipsets; Chip integration, about the chipsets:

pg 91-**About the Integrated and connected ICs**

Cleaning the Laptop and Its Importance

pg 91-**Cleaning the Laptop and Its Importance**

pg 92-**Proper Screen Cleaning Method**

pg 92-**Cleaning the Inside of the Laptop**

pg 93-**Cleaning the Outside of the Laptop**

pg 93-**Cleaning the Keyboard**

pg 94-**Cleaning the Optical Drives Optical Lens (CD/DVD)**

The Laptops BIOS

The Laptops BIOS; Editing the settings:

pg 94-**Flashing the BIOS, Editing, Updating and Troubleshooting**

The Tools Used To Repair Laptops

The Tools Used To Repair Laptops; Hand Tools and Power Tools:

pg 95-**Hand Tools Used**

pg 95-**Power Tools Used**

pg 96-**Electronic Testing Equipment Used**

Integrated/Onboard Video Chip (GPU) Repair

Integrated/Onboard Video Chip (GPU) Repair; Graphics/Video/GPU can fail due to Thermal Damage:

pg 97-**About the BGA**

pg 97-**Reflowing the GPU**

pg 104-**Removing the Chip Sealant**

pg 104-**The Coin Stack – Used in the Reflow Process, A KEY INSTRUMENT IN VIDEO CHIP REPAIR**

External Video/GPU Card Repair

External Video/GPU Card Repair; Video cards are common in laptops and are removable:

pg 105-**Repairing the Laptops Video Card, Repairing the Desktops Video Card**

Laptop Case Disassembly

Laptop Case Disassembly; A General Guideline and Summary to Disassembling Any Laptop:

pg 108-**There is a Method to a Laptop Breakdown, Case Removal, Which will apply to any Make or Model Laptop or Notebook, I will explain....**

pg 111-**Disassembling the Screen**

pg 112-**Removing the screen from the lower base assembly**

pg 112-**Removing the Palmrest**

pg 112-**The Hinge Cover**

Soldering

Soldering; Tools and equipment used for laptop soldering:

pg 113-**Soldering gun vs. Soldering wand vs. soldering station**

pg 113-**Types of solder to use on Laptop Motherboards**

Soldering; **Types of Fluxes and their uses:**

pg 113-**Rosin Paste Flux and its use**

pg 114-**Liquid (no residue) Flux and its use**

Soldering; **Desoldering (removing components):**

pg 114-**Desoldering pumps and their uses**

pg 115-**Desoldering braid, or Solder wick/Solder braid**

pg 115-**Using Flux for easier removal or components or parts that are soldered onto the motherboard**

pg 115-**The Desoldering Process**

Soldering; **How to Solder (soldering components):**

pg 116-**Adding solder before removing the solder, here's why…**

pg 117-**Holding the tip to the contact point to create "flow"**

pg 117-**Soldering a new trace contact pad or planer ring**

pg 121-**The Soldering Process**

Software Issues and Repair How-To

Software Issues and Repair How-To; **Blue Screen Issues:**

pg 123-**Blue screen issues**

OPERATING SYSTEM NOT INSTALLING

OPERATING SYSTEM NOT INSTALLING; **SATA DRIVE NOT RECOGNIZED ISSUE:**

pg 125-**Configuring the BIOS**

pg 126-**APPLE BOOT KEY COMBINATIONS**

Introduction:

This book was written due to the demand for a clearer understanding into how exactly a laptop works. Laptop, Notebook, Netbook and other Portable Computer Repairing is not a skill yet taught in Classes, Colleges or in the Industry. Until now, Laptop Repairing is/was learned by watching videos on the web, reading forum discussion boards or by simply not repairing and just replacing the part due to lack of knowledge on the subject in question.

I hope to share my repair knowledge of over 21 years of board level laptop and notebook repairing experience with everyone to teach the correct methods of repair and give the aspiring Technician or hobbyist the know-how to successfully complete any repair issue that may arise.

Related Certifications: Computer Fundamentals, (windows XP) June 2006, Computer Technical Support, November 2006, Computer Fundamentals (Mac OSx 10.4), November 2004, Computer Forensics (U.S.), January 2000, Internet Research Techniques and Resources (U.S.), June 2003, Cisco Network Support, September 2005, Computer Literacy, (Windows XP) May 2002, A+ Certification, February 2003, Recert in June 2009, CCNA, August 2000

Learning laptop repair and being proficient at it, requires knowledge in both electronic and science fields as well as the IT field.

Page | 14

Garry Romaneo

Understanding Laptops

THE LAPTOPS EXTERIOR

The Laptops Exterior; the Keyboard:

Replacing a missing key:

The typical key on a laptop keyboard will consist of the plastic key cap itself, and then under the key cap is a plastic hinge retainer set, usually having 2 parts. They snap onto the top key pad and also lock and snap onto the keyboard lower pad. You can also find metal hinge bracing bar attached to the key, these are commonly used on double sized keys to help support the key and stabilize it. The Key will also have a rubber cap in the center, located on the key pad itself and covering the contact pad for that individual key, this is used to touch the pad on the keyboard to register that specific key... as it will expand and contract when depressed... taking its original shape and ready for the next depression. Assuming the hinge set is in good shape, and the post connection rails on the keyboard pad are functioning and not broken, you can snap the key back onto the keyboard. To do so, you will start from the bottom end of the key (the side closest to you), you will notice on the keypad that there is a curved metal hinge holder, the lower hinge bar will slide upward into this and the upper part of the key will snap downward onto the key pad. Sometimes it is side to side and not bottom to top... in this case, you look to see which side has the curved bracket and start there, sliding the hinge bar in and snapping the other end down onto the pad.

Replacement keys can sometimes be found on EBay, this is useful if you only need to replace one or two keys, though can be costly and not worth it if in need of numerous key replacement. Keys will average around $6.00 *USD* and Keyboards average around $20.00 *USD,* so beyond needing 3 or more keys, it is more economical to simply replace the whole keyboard. If you are a repair technician, you will want to save any broken or non-functional keyboard, you can use these for future key replacements, saving the need for ordering a specific key if ever needed.

Repairing a Key

First, you will need to check the keypad metal braces as these are what hold the key securely to the keypad. There are typically 4 individual post hinge braces, usually with two of them being loop shaped (hollow center), and the other one or 2 being bent (hook) shaped. You need to look closely to see if the 2 loop braces are seated straight upward at a 90 degree angle, if not, then you need to use needle nosed or a micro sized flat head screwdriver to straighten this brace. If this loop brace or the latch/hook brace are even slightly bent, they can fail to properly lock the key down. If however you determine any one of these 4 braces to be broken, then a new keyboard will be needed, these braces cannot be repaired once broken, and if one of the three is broke, the other three will not properly lock the key down and it will continue to pop off the pad. If the rubber contact cap should fall off, you will need to reseal it to the pad. To do this, you will need epoxy or super glue, applying a small amount to the lip of the rubber cap, then, placing it back in position over the contact pad. Some keyboards will allow you to simply rest the rubber cap over the contact pad and it will stay there once the key is reattached due to an indent in the keypad where the cap can rest securely.

How the keyboard connects to the motherboard

A typical laptop keyboard will use a ribbon style cable, which will connect to a Slot style port on the motherboard. The cables plug end will lock down into the port on the motherboard, and there are 2 common types of port lock tabs. Another style of keyboard has the connection port located on the bottom side of the keyboard and it slides into the port in the palmrest, which travels by ribbon cable onto the motherboard.

FLIP DOWN style keyboard input port, which has a plastic flap that flips up to unlock and flips down to lock, you can use a guitar pick to pry the flap upward to unlock it and release the ribbon cable…

The second style uses two locking plastic tabs on either side of the port, the tabs are slid upward (not up toward you, rather, up toward the screen). Unlock both sides, only sliding them upward a few millimeters, do not pull too hard or they will break or pop off. If this happens, try to re-snap them back in/on. The Keyboard ribbon cable will either slide into the locking port, or it will snap onto the port.

The Laptops Exterior; the Touchpad:

Repairing broken buttons

The touchpad buttons are usually connected to the palmrest using plastic braces. These braces will attach to the palmrest using plastic rivets (melted plastic caps), and if the buttons are pressed on a lot or over extended when depressed, those plastic securing rivets can break, causing the button to "flop" around inside the button bay.

To repair the braces to the palmrest, you can melt new plastic caps onto the braces. Use the solder gun to quickly heat the plastic, you can use a pen cap or similar as your plastic source. You will touch the plastic being used to recap the brace, and hold on the rivet location, touch the solder gun tip onto the plastic and it will melt quickly. Press down and twist the plastic away quickly, you should be left with a new plastic cap, if not, repeat. Be careful here not to melt or warp the actual bracing that attaches to the button, it will not be repairable as it will weaken the plastic. You will need to replace or repair any broken or missing rubber caps if there are any used. Some laptop models do use these rubber cap button inserts, and some do not use them.

Replacing or Repairing the Touchpad

Touchpads rarely fail; they take quite a beating and can withstand minor liquid spills without failure. Though, on rare occasion, they can fail. If you encounter touchpad failure the first thing to do is to rule out a software or driver conflict. Uninstall existing and reinstall the drivers for the touchpad. Next, you would check the circuit board that is attached to the underside of the palmrest, looking for liquid damage, or blown components. Finally, you will inspect the ribbon cables that run from the touchpad to the circuit controller board and the cable that runs from the circuit board down to the motherboard, ensuring there are no breaks in the fine-fragile ribbon cable. You can find replacement touchpad assemblies on EBay or similar, though before purchasing one, make sure you also price out a Palmrest that will include the touchpad, sometimes they are equal in price and the palmrest could be in better condition than your existing one, allowing you to gain a free upgrade without spending any more than you would have only buying the touchpad assembly insert.

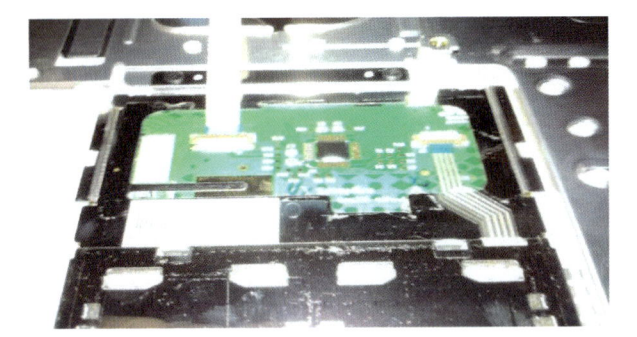

Using the built in features on the Touchpad

Touchpads will typically have slider strips located on the edges of the sides or bottom of the touchpad rectangular area. Some laptop models require an add-on driver to recognize this feature and some models load it by default. This scroll bar, slider bar will allow you to quickly scroll up and down pages, which saves a step or two in browsing the screen with the cursor.

Tapping feature is also available for all touchpads. Some will have it disabled by default and will need the settings changed to enable it. What its purpose is, it will allow you to quickly tap on the touchpad finger area and simulate the "right click" buttons feature of executing an action.

The Laptops Exterior; the **Ports, Input and Output Connections on a Laptop**:

VGA/Serial Port/DVI

This is the port where you connect an external monitor to, like a desktop computers screen for example, or with the correct adapter connectors, connection to the TV is possible. It uses a 15 pin female connection port.

HDMI

This port uses a 19 pin or a 29 pin connection, HDMI stands for High Definition Multimedia Interface. This allows for higher quality resolutions, higher frame-rates which are required on most new TVs like the LED LCD, HDTV, Plasma and alike.

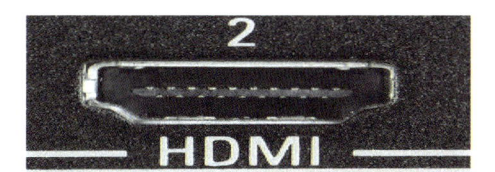

FireWire

For windows users, this will be a port rarely used, though it has high speed capability and can be used for peripherals such as media devices, hard drives and optical drives.

S-Video

This is typically a circular 7 pin video port and is commonly used for passing the laptop screen viewing onto the Television screen

Printer Port - parallel port

This uses a 25 pin female connection port, and is used rarely in newer laptops, yet it will be found on all older models. It is used to connect a printer or even a Fax Machine to.

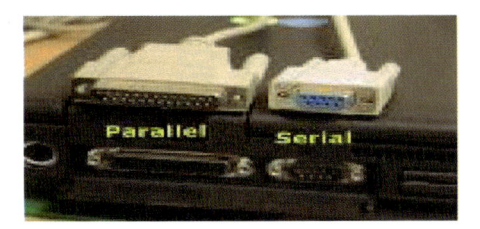

Docking Station Port

These ports will usually be found on the bottom or the rear of the laptop, and typically only the laptop models that were released as "business" laptops or notebooks were equipped with one. They allow connection to a Base Station that houses all the same ports that a typical laptop and desktop computer will have on it, including other extra ports. It allows you to connect all peripherals permanently, while allowing you to connect and disconnect the laptop without having to reconnect the cables every time. The laptop or notebook computer will simply snap into place and lock itself in securely.

USB

Probably the most commonly used port on the laptop, used to power devices and peripherals. Its ease of use and high transfer rates make it a must have component of every laptop in existence. The current available SATA devices use SATA1 (black), SATA2 (white) or SATA3 (blue). You can tell which is which by the color of the plastic pin tray inside the plug tip port.

Audio Out/Headphone Jack Port

This port is where you will plug in any external headphones or speakers, the individual ports will be labeled with icons that indicate which port is which.

PC Card Slot, Remote Control Slot, SD Slot

Wireless cards will plug into this port, Camera cards, Camera memory cards, and remote controls that are included with some laptops, mainly the "entertainment center" laptops.

Ethernet/Modem Port

This is where you will plug in your DSL or Ethernet cable for internet access; it is faster than wireless and keeps constant signal strength.

The modem port is used less these days; it was commonly used for internet access, more commonly known as "dial up" access. Due to speed restrictions, this is not used unless it is the only choice available.

The Laptops Exterior: The Palmrest:

Repairing broken screw posts

This is actually a very common issue among all the laptop makes and models. It usually happens due to screws vibrating loose and never getting re-tightened or due to over-tightening the screw. The screw post consists of 2 parts, the post itself, which is molded into the palmrests undercarriage. And the Screw Grip insert, which is typically gold in color and is heat set into place from the factory. This screw insert nut has a serrated edge on the outside of it, which seals the nut to the post and prevents friction slippage. Being that it is only heat seated into a plastic post, after time or by use of excessive force, the plastic to metal contact can "strip" and either the screw nut will spin freely or it will fall out of the screw post.

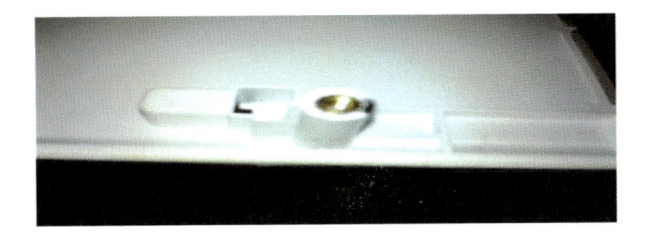

You can use a Plastic-Metal epoxy to repair this post, this epoxy can easily be purchased at any Hobby store, or electronics store, or even an auto parts store. It is a two-part glue, and once mixed it is placed quickly onto the part before the setting process sets in. It is best to use a toothpick or similar for this project because it is thin and can help to shape the epoxy once applied.

Once you apply a fair amount of the epoxy, you can reseat the broken post back onto its base (assuming you still have the post), If no post is left, you will have to attempt to reshape one, use your best judgment on shaping it and make it look exactly like the others. You will need to let the epoxy set up a little to form a shape that will hold, then once slightly hardened and in the proper shape, you can set the screw insert nut into the makeshift post. Align the screw nut so that the screw inserted will catch the threads and work properly. Curing time will be roughly 6 to 12 hours, though there are different cure times for every brand of epoxy.

Replacing the Palmrest

When replacing the palmrest due to damage or cosmetic appearance, you will need to get an exact replacement part. There usually are no compatible upgradeable or swappable replacements, though you will find some series of the same manufacturer use similar palmrest configurations that are interchangeable. For instance, a Dell Inspiron E1505 palmrest will fit onto a 1501 base with a-little modifying. If you simply remove the plastic cross bard to fit the front button panel, the palmrest will fit and the button and led lights will work. But, to play it safe, always order the exact model of palmrest needed, there are stickers on the underside of the palmrest to indicate the Part number, if not, you will order by the laptops model part number.

Buttons or Switches on the Palmrest

The most common button on the palmrest is the power on/off button, its location will vary from laptop to laptop depending on whatever design the manufacturer chooses, there is no "set" place for the button. Other common buttons on a laptops palmrest are Media buttons, which include the pause, record, rewind, fast forward and the stop buttons. Wireless on and off switches are sometimes placed in the palmrest housing, and the screen sleep switch is located on the palmrest if there is one, most newer laptops will use magnets to activate the sleep switch.

The Laptops Exterior: The Screen:

The Layers of a laptops screen and their purposes

The front layer is the glass liquid crystal display panel, it is the part that produces the image, it however does not house the lighting, it instead refracts the lighting given off by the backpanel. The middle layers consist of polarizing films and reflective films. Followed by the backpanel, which is white in color, it bounces the white light outward towards the liquid crystal display panel to illuminate the pixels.

How the screen works

The LCD or LED bulb(s) are typically located on the bottom and shine upward, though some laptops also have side lighting and upper lighting. The LCD Bulb fits over the backpanel and a layer of reflective film and a thick plastic panel, if this is not seated completely level like it originally came, it will produce light leaks and you will see light spots on the front side of the screen when viewing. If seated properly, the bulb light will shine straight up the reflective film panel and the thick plastic panel and when doing so, the light being directed in reverse towards the white backpanel then it bounces off the backpanel illuminating the front LCD panel which in turn lights up the image being produced by the liquid crystal display.

LED vs. LCD (ccfl)

LED lighting is the newer of the two backlight options, it will have a longer lifespan, it will produce brighter more evenly spread out light, and it will consume less power, therefor making it a better and cheaper choice, which is why virtually all the current laptops being manufactured will have LED lighting installed. LCD light is sufficient as we have been used to it since the birth of the laptop, it is fairly simple to obtain replacement parts for both bulbs and inverters, making it a solid choice. Currently it is easier to determine the faulty component on an LCD screen as opposed to determining the faulty component on an LED screen, usually you will end up replacing the whole screen when failure occurs being that LED screens are a bit more touchy and can cause further damage to other components if alteration occurs or the wrong screen is attached. LED is by far the better choice for viewing; there is really no comparison between the two. LED viewing gives you full brightness and no dark areas, images appear clearer and crisper images are viewable.

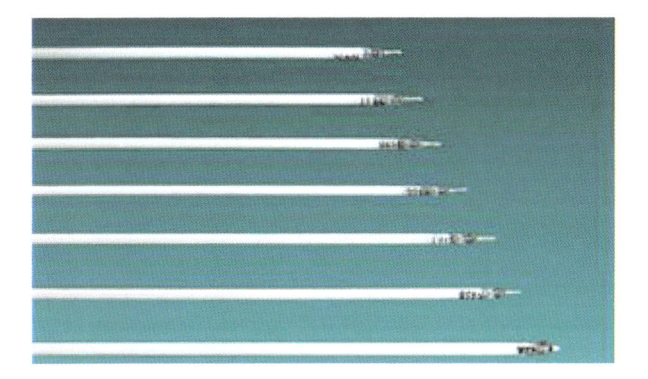

Signs of a cracked screen, what to look for

When a fracture or crack occur in the screens glass front panel, it will usually start out as a small chip or crack, but will soon grow, it always does. It will spread out like a spider web until it reaches the opposite end, then you will also notice a black oily looking appearance to the areas where the cracks are. The oily look is due to pressure being applied to the sensitive LCD panel pixels. There is no replacing or repairing a cracked screen, it must be replaced as it is attached permanently to the screens back circuit panel and is not a swappable part.

Determining Failure to the screens circuit panel board

Screen flexing is the number one cause of damage to the screens back panel circuit board. It takes a lot of abuse from the lid being opened and closed numerous times. With manufacturers always trying to make the laptops lighter, they use a lighter, thinner plastic for the screens housing. This circuit board panel had more built in protection in the earlier model laptops, because their main concern wasn't how much it weighed, they were concentrating on speeding them up. They used a thicker plastic housing on the older models, even adding metal bracing panels to give added support.

Pressure points will also damage this circuit board panel, for example, if someone uses their thumb to open and close the lid continuously and when doing so, they apply beyond the amount of force needed, they can push indentations into the panel and can cause component failure, contact pad cracks and faults, blown fuses and more. You will usually not be able to repair this back circuit panel unless you can visually see a blown component. The fault usually occurs within the layers of the circuit board and cannot be repaired.

Replacing the screen

Screen replacement is one of the most common repairs done to a laptop, and one of the more costly repairs. Some screens are interchangeable, meaning that the same screen will work in several different models and series, and some laptops must use an exact part replacement. When in doubt, it is best to get an exact replacement, and to do this, you need to get the number off of the back of the screen, the part number. The part number will look something like this: LTN156AT05, and if you look at the number it tells you the screen size in it. In this case, the size of the screen is 15.6 inch. The numbers following the screen size on the part number need to match exactly for the screen to function properly. If the wrong one is attached, it can cause white outs on the screen, sometimes not appearing for days or weeks. Or worse, it can blow the components on the motherboard or the port connection can short out.

To remove the screen, you first will remove the plastic front bezel, or the screen frame (see the screen repair section for directions on removing the front bezel). Once the bezel is off, you will see that the screen is attached to side support rails, you will next look for the screws on this rail and remove them (usually 2 to 4). Then look to the top of the screen on the top edges and in the top center, remove any retaining screws here. Now, if there is a webcam above the screen, you will unplug the cable from the webcam circuit panel board. You can now pull the screen forward from the top pulling it to lay face down onto the palmrest/keyboard area, go slow here and look for any cables or wires that might prevent you from lying the screen down onto the palmrest area. You can place a paper towel or a foam pad down first, to prevent possible scratching to the surface of the screen. Now you need to unplug the LCD wire assembly and plug from the power inverter (unless it's an LED screen), then you will unplug the display cable from the back of the screen. To unplug the display cable from the screen, they add a sticky plastic tape tab to the display cable plug end, this will have to be unpeeled to remove the cable from the port, and do not pull the tape all the way off, it is meant to also be used an a grip handle to help pull the cable safely from the port. Some display cables use 2 prongs to lock it into the display cable input port on the screen; you will notice 2 small lever looking tabs on either end of the display cable. You squeeze both sides simultaneously while pulling in a downward motion to slide the cable away from the input port, to reinsert you simply snap it back in place.

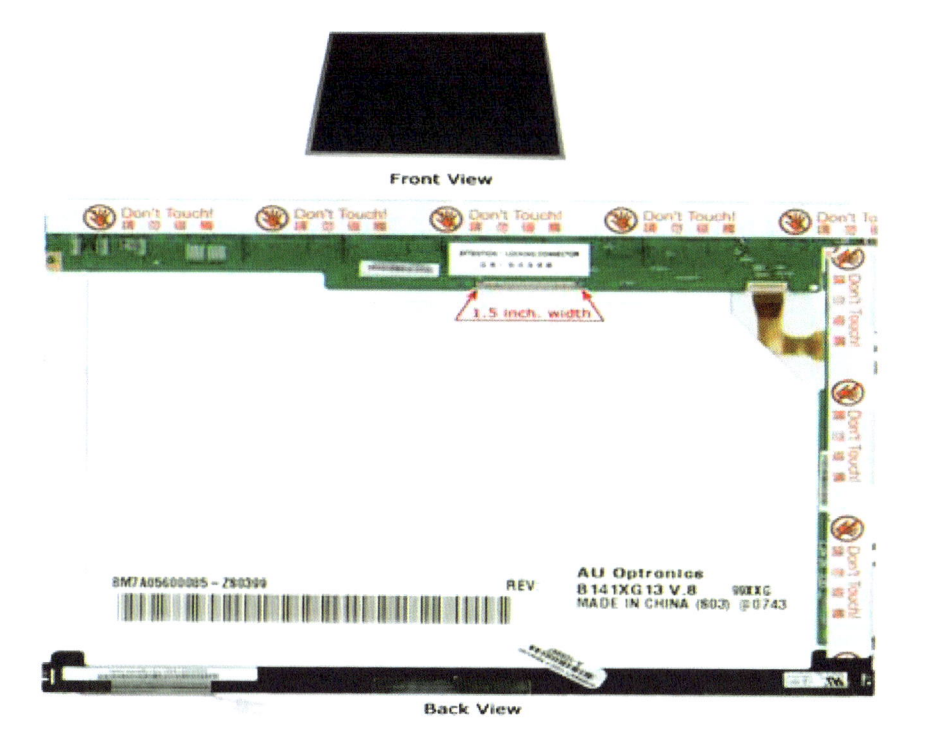

The best place to locate an exact replacement screen is EBay, you simply type the part number into the search box, choose a reputable seller and always read that sellers negative feedback to determine if it is safe to buy from them. If you end up getting a "bad" screen it can sometimes take weeks to get the defective screen replaced from the seller and can be a big pain. Though nowadays, EBay and PayPal has become a lot more buyer friendly and they guarantee every purchase made, meaning, if a seller for some reason scams you, EBay will pay you and they then take up the dispute with your seller and leave you with no need for future recourse.

Tablet PC Screens

Don't let the appearance scare you, they are basically the same screen as a normal laptop screen, they just use an extra layer on top of the LCD glass panel. They will have a digitizer panel, it is touch sensitive to either finger or stylus pen. The housing only differs in that it has a central Hinge located in the center of the base/screen bottom. It is positioned in the middle to allow the screen to swivel to one side and to allow it to fold over the opposite way, disassembling this screen is still the same as a regular screen.

The digitizer panel, its uses and how to replace

The digitizer panel will be secured to the back cover using screws, you will need to visually locate the securing screws and remove them to remove the digitizer panel from the screen panel. It will usually attach to the screen using a ribbon type cable connection and you must be careful here not to damage the ribbon cable when removing the digitizer. Make sure to unlock the ribbon cable ports locking tab, located on the cable input port before removing the digitizer panel. Once you have removed the digitizer panel, you will notice that now the screen is exactly the same as one that goes in a normal laptop or notebook, if it is damaged, you will repair/replace as you would a normal laptop screen.

The Laptops Exterior: **The Bottom Base – Housing**:

Repairing broken or missing screw posts

The same process is followed as previously discussed in the Palmrest section, you will need to use an epoxy glue to either re-secure the post back onto the base housing, or you will need to build a new one if capable of doing so.

Removing the bottom base from the motherboard

Some manufacturers will secure the motherboard to the upper palm rest, like Sony Vaio, but most laptops are designed with the motherboard being secured to the bottom base housing. This design will keep the motherboard from flexing due to the bottom base housing having a stronger foundation. Sony Vaios will typically incorporate some type of metal bracing to help prevent any flexing issues from occurring. To remove the bottom base from the motherboard, you will need to remove all other parts and components first, taking the laptop down to just the motherboard and bottom base. Now you can remove the motherboard to free the bottom base. Start by removing any securing screws from the motherboard; these are usually labeled and numbered. Next you will unplug any remaining cables or wires to free the board. Grab ahold of the motherboard from the cdrom port area and pry it upward gently, pull it up only about an inch or so, then look on the underside of the board for any connected cables or wires. The HP DV Series laptops will have the dc jack plug connected to the underside of the board, and if not careful, you can rip the port from the motherboard; the Ethernet cable plug is also connected to the underside of the motherboard and will need to be unplugged prior to removing the motherboard. Also you should look at the fan securing screws, on some models; the 2 screws need to be removed to separate the motherboard from the base. Now continue lifting the motherboard in an upward tilted motion and if nothing else is restricting its removal, go ahead and remove the motherboard, if however the board still seems to be attached, you must carefully inspect the motherboard for any remaining securing screws or cable connections and finish removing them, do not force the motherboard out.

Replacing the bottom base

If you need to replace the bottom base, you must purchase an exact replacement base. These are typically sold in grades or ascending quality, starting from Grade A down to Grade C, A being near new, C being used/work/scratched. The price will be reflective of the grade given to the part, you will probably want a New or Grade A part when replacing simply because you do not know the history of usage on any used part being sold to you and that base can be weakened or a hairline fracture that went unnoticed can worsen causing part failure and re-replacement. Once again, EBay is the place to get a replacement base; you will enter the laptops make and model into the search box. For example: Gateway MA3 Bottom Base… and your results will be for that specific series with corresponding photos to look at and zoom in on to ensure the part is the same.

The Laptops Exterior: The Access Areas on the Underside of a Laptop:

Hard Drive Cover

This port cover will usually be rectangular in shape and right around 3 inches wide by 4 to 5 inches long, secured to the bottom base with one to four screws. There will usually be an indented access area for you to fit a pry tool or a fingernail into to pry the cover upward and away from the base. These are the most common hard drive covers, the other type are pre-attached to the hard drive to allow you to grab ahold and slide the hard drive in and out of the port, and the drive is moved to the side of the laptop with the cover wrapping from the side to the bottom of the laptop. The securing screws on this type are usually located on the underside of the laptop and usually will use 2 screws, these screws are thicker than any other screw used on the laptop.

RAM Cover

The RAM cover is a small rectangular shaped plastic tray; it will usually have an imprinted icon marking its location. Its purpose it to allow easy access to the RAM sticks and the DIMM slot(s). Remember, the RAM might be split up, having one port on the bottom side of the motherboard and the second port located on the upper side of the motherboard (usually beneath the keyboard)

Wi-Fi Cover

This cover will usually be a smaller square to shaped plastic cover, also located on the bottom of the laptop for easy access to the wireless card and antenna wires. The shape might be different if the laptop has more than just a WLAN card, if it also has a WWAN or SSD or similar port, it will usually stretch the cover to fit the opening shape needed. The Wi-Fi port cover will typically have an imprinted icon to label its location, same as the hard drive usually will have one too.

Optical Drive Plate/Cover

This is a snap on piece, and on older models they use both snaps and screws to secure it to the disc tray. It is not a replaceable part as it is proprietary to its specific drive tray. It is however repairable if it happens to break off. The average drive cover will have 3 securing snap tabs and if one happens to break off you can simply apply some contact cement or super glue to the area where the tab broke and it will secure it back onto the drive tray. If you can replace the part because you have a similar cdrom, you would simply unsnap the cover and re-snap the replacement into place.

CPU/Heatsink Cover

You will not find this on every laptop, as it will only be available on certain models. It is convenient for the average home user to be able to access the heatsink radiator fins and allow cleaning of the parts. This in turn will allow the laptop to stay cool and prevent overheating. What you will usually find when removing this cover is the heatsink, you will remove the four retaining spring screws and pry the heatsink off to gain access to the CPU or fan assembly area.

The Laptops Exterior: The Access Areas on the Underside of a Laptop:

Hard Drive, Battery and Power on/off lights and their locations

These are usually found at the front of the palmrest and there can be a secondary or even third set located on the hinge cover and/or the media strip panel above the keyboard area. These lighted icons can be useful for troubleshooting and for general reference as to how the laptop is currently running. The lights can also change color to indicate different stated of that hardware. Take the battery lighted icon for example... If the battery is drained and at "low Battery", the battery light color will typically change, and instead of a solid lighted bulb, it will rapidly blink on and off indicating it needs to charge. It will sometimes show a different color if you plug in the AC Adapter an opposed to being on battery power alone.

The Laptops Battery and All About it

Laptop Battery Tips

How Does a Laptop Battery Work?

Laptop batteries house internal power cells that are laid parallel to one another. A circuit board inside the battery manages the recharge and discharge of the battery. Cells are regulated by the circuit board to ensure that the battery is never overcharged, and that each cell drains in equal amount. Hardware inside the laptop ensures that the battery is working properly, and displays an icon on the monitor to indicate the performance of the battery. On a chemical level, the laptop battery is rechargeable, and undergoes electro chemical reaction and reduction at the positive and negative terminals. This simply means that the process of the battery during use (electrons flowing in one direction to the end terminal) is reversed in order to recharge the battery (moves the electrons back to the starting terminal). This process can be done repeatedly, because the circuit board in the battery regulates the chemical draining precisely. If the circuit were taken out of the design, the battery would cause a short circuit and wreck the laptop.

Design specifications

Laptop batteries are designed to absolutely conform to the shape, size, weight, and functionality of the laptop. This is why the battery is made by the manufacturer of the laptop. Battery weight must not exceed the weight of the laptop. The battery is designed to fit securely in the laptop battery compartment or chassis. Each laptop model has a different battery designed specifically to weigh and fit the laptop, as well as perform to the specifications of the laptop hardware. Function is the most important element in battery design. The size and function elements of a laptop require a vast difference in battery shapes and sizes.

Life of a battery

Laptop batteries are made with lithium ion/polymer or nickel metal hydride. No matter which kind of battery is in a laptop, that battery will not last forever. When a user plugs the power cable into a laptop, the chemical process of reversing the electrons back to the first terminal begins. This action is normally fine, unless the laptop battery has been nearly drained. A full recharge on a typical laptop battery can be done several hundred times before the battery needs to be replaced. Things that can drain a battery rapidly include using the brightness at full capacity and playing movies from the DVD drive. Video games can run down the battery, especially if the game requires a CD to be in the drive during play.

The Media Strip Lights and Icons

The media strip is almost always placed on the palmrest or upper base area, located just above the keyboard, it can also be located on either side of the keyboard, Toshiba likes to do this placement on some of their older models. In the media strip you can find the power on-off button, sometimes the eject button is placed there, the play/pause/RR/FF buttons are almost always found on the media strip.

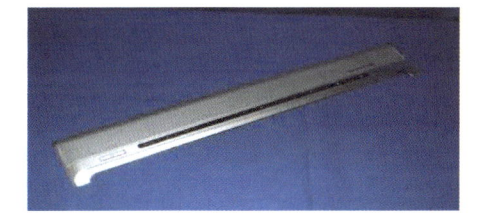

Using Different Colors for the LED Lights and Why

As explained earlier, the power, the cdrom and the hard drive lights will both blink and change color according to its activity. The hard drive Icon (usually an incomplete circle with a vertical line in it) will blink rapidly when the hard drive is in use, or will stay a solid color if hard drive is idling. The power good icon will usually incorporate color change, when it is plugged into AC Adapter power its typical color is solid green (green is standard), and when on battery alone the color will usually change to an orangish-yellow color, then some laptops will use a red or purple to show that both AC Adapter and Battery are plugged in and battery is currently charging.

The Battery Icon will act similar to the power on-off lighted icon. Your manual will give you specifics as to what color means what for your specific laptop make and model.

Laptop Power Sources and Management

Laptop Power Sources and Management; The **AC Adapter (charging cord)**:

The AC cord end, the DC cord end and the power inverter box

The section of cord from the inverter box to the wall socket plug tip is the AC end of the plug. It takes the 110/220 volts and converts the power from alternating current to direct current at the power inverter box. Then from the power inverter box to the plug tip, it is DC current, and can be a variety of different voltages depending on the specific model of laptop, the most common today being 19v or 19 volts, 3.4 amps . Pets seem particularly fond of the DC end of the cords, they seem to know to stay away from the AC end where the High Voltage is, I am assuming this is due to the high pitch buzzing noise that the adapter can give off.

Testing the AC Adapter

You should start by doing a thorough examination of the cable, looking for crimps, breaks or knots in the cable. When knots are present, the possibility exists for the negative grounding twisted wire to touch the insulated power wire(s) and create a short in the connection. Next area to look at closely at is the AC Adapter plug tip and the cable going into the plug end. This is a common area of failure because it receives a lot of movement from plugging and unplugging the cord into the jack port. If you hold the plug tip in one hand and the cable in the other, grabbing the cable right where it meets the plug, then slightly wiggle the cable and plug to listen for a cracking or snapping sound which would indicate a broken connection in the plug housing.

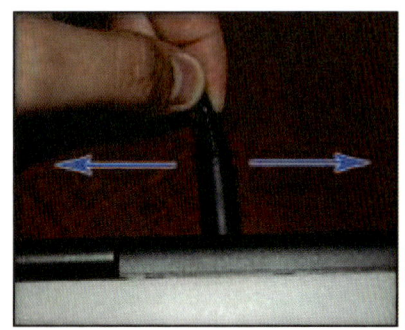

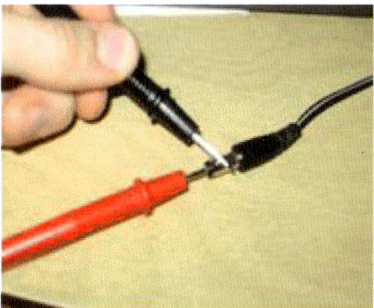

Now you should use your multimeter to test power to the tip. To do this, you power on the multimeter and attach the negative probe (black) to the outside of the plug tip metal. You attach the positive probe (red) to the inside of the plug (if your multimeters probe spike is too thick to insert it into the plugs tip hole, then you can attach a paperclip or similar to your probe by wrapping it around the probe a few times and then extending a straight piece to use as your probe extension). Test for the correct Power by reading the voltage output, or set the multimeter to beep when power is attached to do a quick "power good" test.

Repairing the Cord

If the fault in the cable is in the cabling itself and not the inverter box or the plug tip, you will determining the possible fault area, and cut the cable a few millimeters before the supposed fault, and one more cut on the other side of the cable about the same length from the fault, this will ensure you have nice clean breaks from both ends. You will peel the insulating rubber from the top layer of wire. This top layer will be the ground layer and is usually twisted or braided for less interference. Pull the wire casing back about a half inch, and do the same for the other wire end. You will now untwist or unbraid the outer layer of wire, then twist it tight to make it all one single thick wire. You will see another wire or even 2 more wires that have insulating in the middle of the cable, these are the power wired, you will remove a small portion of the insulating rubber on it as well… Try to make your wire tips all start from different parts along the wire, this way gives it less of a chance that it will make contact with another wire and makes for a thinner bunch if wire in the end.

Get yourself some wire shrink tubing if available (electronics or auto stores) as it will create a more professional repair than using standard electrical tape. Cut small pieces that are slightly larger than the wire itself and slide them onto the wire but keep them far enough from any heat to prevent them from prematurely shrinking. You will also need a large tube to put over the wire set, this will cover all your finished work be recreating an outer insulating cover, you will slide this piece over all the individual wires you just repaired to seal and strengthen your repair area. You will heat your solder gun now and tin the tip. Apply flux paste/gel to each wire end (both sides), and apply some solder to the tip of the soldering gun. You will need a medium size teardrop of solder on the tip per wire connection. Hold the two matching wires overlapping one another, and then apply the solder gun tip to the wire ends; you want to hold the tip into the wire for a few seconds to ensure the solder reaches "liquid state" and achieves "flow". Then pull the solder gun wand away quickly and cool the wires, Slide the heat shrink tubing over the repair area and heat it to shrink fit it. Lastly, you will slide the large piece of heat shrink tubing over the whole repaired area and heat to seal.

Repairing the Plug Tip

The same method would apply to the plug and tip area, except you will use a razor blade to cut away the thick plastic plug material to expose the wires and to be able to repair the fault.

To repair the AC Adapter, you will use a razor to cut away the hard plastic/rubber plug end… I usually will cut up to where it bends, or on the ones with a straight tip, I will cut up to where the metal plug portion ends inside the plug tip…

Make a cut the whole way around the cord/plug… then make 1 or 2 cuts downward to the end of the plug cap…You should be able to peel off the plug hard cap… exposing the wires inside..

There are typically 2 wires… though some Adapters have 3 or more…

You need to make note of this and keep them separated from one another.

The most common 2 wire cable will have a main wire, the center wire, and it will be insulated... usually with a white wire coating... then the negative wire will be braided around the entire outside of this main center wire...The Braiding will give better grounding capability and less fault interruption interference.

When repairing these 2 wires, you will want to expose at least an inch on either side of the break for repair and resealing...

Then Clip both wires, You can usually clip the whole cable with 1 snip, then cut away some of the wire cover, then you would gather all the outer silver grounding wire and twist that into a single wire (a tight twist)... Then take the center wire, cut the shielding on it... but cut that one a little shorter so that they positive and negative wires are not exposed and to avoid the possibility of them touching together at the point where they are exposed.

Re-twist all wire ends (4) and Get the Solder gun hot....

You will need to first cut yourself some Heat Shrink Tubing to Use in the wires... Size yourself up a piece... NOTE: that when buying Heat Shrink Tubing you should get the variety size pack...

They can be bought at Most Retail Auto Stores, Or Electronics Stores...

Slip the Heat Shrink Tubing Over the Wires... only do it from one side... and slide it back enough that the heat from the soldering iron will not heat the tubing prematurely... Then you will want to apply Flux Paste to the wire tips, and do it to all 4 wire ends...

Then Tin your Soldering Iron and Apply solder to the tip.... You will now solder the two wire sections together... then slide the heat shrink tubing over your soldered wire areas and heat to shrink the tubing and seal the repair...

Note: I will sometimes use two or more different sizes in tubing at the same time... I will start out by adding the first tube... the first added will be slightly larger than the cable itself... then I will slip on a slightly larger one and slide it on top of the first... then a third... Then ... when the wires are soldered ... you slip the tightest one first over the repair... heat it to shrink it... then the second tightest gets slid on top of the first... heated and continue on to the third... then Finish off by heating one last time to ensure it is sealed and snug.... You will have a thicker/stronger repair if more than one layer of tubing is used...

Laptop Power Sources and Power Management; The Battery:

Proper Usage Tips

ALL ABOUT THE LAPTOPS BATTERY

Laptop Battery Tips

How Does a Laptop Battery Work?

Laptop batteries house internal power cells that are laid parallel to one another. A circuit board inside the battery manages the recharge and discharge of the battery. Cells are regulated by the circuit board to ensure that the battery is never overcharged, and that each cell drains in equal amount. Hardware inside the laptop ensures that the battery is working properly, and displays an icon on the monitor to indicate the performance of the battery. On a chemical level, the laptop battery is rechargeable, and undergoes electro chemical reaction and reduction at the positive and negative terminals. This simply means that the process of the battery during use (electrons flowing in one direction to the end terminal) is reversed in order to recharge the battery (moves the electrons back to the starting terminal). This process can be done repeatedly, because the circuit board in the battery regulates the chemical draining precisely. If the circuit were taken out of the design, the battery would cause a short circuit and wreck the laptop.

Design specifications

Laptop batteries are designed to absolutely conform to the shape, size, weight, and functionality of the laptop. This is why the battery is made by the manufacturer of the laptop. Battery weight must not exceed the weight of the laptop. The battery is designed to fit securely in the laptop battery compartment or chassis. Each laptop model has a different battery designed specifically to weigh and fit the laptop, as well as perform to the specifications of the laptop hardware. Function is the most important element in battery design. The size and function elements of a laptop require a vast difference in battery shapes and sizes.

Determining Failure and Drainage of the Battery

Laptop batteries are made with lithium ion/polymer or nickel metal hydride. No matter which kind of battery is in a laptop, that battery will not last forever. When a user plugs the power cable into a laptop, the chemical process of reversing the electrons back to the first terminal begins. This action is normally fine, unless the laptop battery has been nearly drained. A full recharge on a typical laptop battery can be done several hundred times before the battery needs to be replaced. Things that can drain a battery rapidly include using the brightness at full capacity and playing movies from the DVD drive. Video games can run down the battery, especially if the game requires a CD to be in the drive during play.

Replacing the Battery

When replacing a Laptop battery, you do not necessarily have to use the part number from the battery itself; you just use the laptops model number to find a battery. Either look on the laptops front screen frame for the model number, or look on the bottom of the laptop for a sticker indicating the model number. Then go on EBay and type the laptop model number and battery after to get results for your laptop. You should also add the text: OEM or Original for better results and an Original Battery replacement instead of a generic "knock-off" model. You will usually be able to choose from different size batteries, in case you choose to upgrade the charge time. You will have options of 6 cell, 9 cell, 12 cell and so on... the larger the number, the greater the batteries charge time, the longer it will last. They will also sometimes offer a raised battery that will lift up the rear when installed; I highly recommend these types as they also do a great deal of good for the cooling of the laptop. There is a big price difference between the generic batteries and the Original batteries, you will also know if it is a "real" battery because the manufacturer's logo will be stamped on it. The average price today for a replacement battery is between $30.00*USD and* $60,00*USD*, generic will cost between $10.00*USD* and $20.00*USD*.

Laptop Power Sources and Power Management; Managing **the Power Settings in Windows**:

Navigating to the Power Settings in Windows

Windows XP, Vista and Windows 7: From the desktop, click on the Start button on the lower left side of the screen, from the list that pops up, navigate to the right column and select – Control Panel... Your control panel window will pop up, from there you will look to the left column of that window and select – Classic View (selecting this will show all the icons in the Control Panel, Otherwise if not selected, it will show groups in the right side of the window. Now navigate to the icon labeled – Power. In here you can edit and tweak the power settings. Please note, these settings might be limited if your laptop is using a 3rd party Power Management Utility. Acer is a common brand that always uses a Power Management Utility, IBM is another, and you will need to go into their management settings to alter the Power Settings.

Another thing to note here is that if you have your Display settings optimized for "performance" rather than "quality" the desktop appearance will be set to "basic" and the Start Button options will appear differently. You would then still Click on the Start button, then still navigate to the Right hand list or column in the pop up window, then you will hover the mouse over the "Settings" text... A secondary window will pop up, and you will choose Control Panel from that list.

Optimizing the Power Settings

Windows XP will by default be configured to use the power scheme "Home/Office Desk", which normally will prevent Windows from throttling the CPU. One can change or configure the power scheme by using Power Options from the Control Panel:

•Minimal Power Management - Will enable CPU throttling if having installed the relevant processor driver

•Always On - Will disable CPU throttling, and keep the CPU's at max power

To disable throttling of the CPU completely in Windows XP without regard to Power Schemes

[HKEY_LOCAL_MACHINE \SYSTEM \CurrentControlSet \Control \Session Manager]

PerfEnablePackageIdle = 0

Preinstalled Power Management Software and Drivers

Some manufacturers will preinstall their own Power Management Software; it will sometimes be bundles with other software management tools.

Laptop Power Sources and Power Management; Power Options in BIOS Setup:

Configuring and Location

Power management is the master control for the four power saving modes, doze, stand by, suspend mode and HDD power down mode. This field allows you to select the type of power saving management mode. Usually there are four selections for power management. In order to use CPU overheat protection the power management option should be enabled.

Disabled: No power management support.

User Define: Users can define their own power management. Each of the ranges is from one minute to one hour, except for HDD power down which ranges from one minute to fifteen minutes.

Min Saving: Predefined timer values are in their MAX values, one hour, one hour, one hour and fifteen minutes respectively.

Max. Saving: Predefined timer values are in their MIN value, one minute.

Laptop RAM or Memory Types

Laptop RAM (random access memory) or Memory Types; DDR 1-DDR 2-DDR 3, microDimm:

The most commonly used Memory

Today's faster laptops will all use DDR3 RAM, though the most common used would be DDR2 RAM. It is the cheapest of the choices due to its availability and being the typical size and speed RAM installed by the manufacturer. MicroDIMM is out dated and not used anymore, the only laptops I can think of offhand that used this RAM is the Panasonic Toughbook. Despite its name you would think it the smallest of the RAM choices, though its width is double that of the typical RAM stick. DDR1 is still around and still pretty common in laptops, though the older laptops are the ones you will find this installed in. Its appearance is the very same as DDR2 and DDR3 RAM the only noticeable difference is the pin counts of each.

Laptop RAM (random access memory) or Memory Types; Types of RAM, Pin Counts and speeds:

Dedicated RAM, Integrated RAM

Laptop memory for the most part will be dedicated, meaning that you will add RAM to ports on the motherboard, and it is not physically attached. It is a better choice because it is upgradable, exchangeable, and doesn't take up needed room on the motherboard. Integrated RAM is just as it is named, integrated into the motherboard. There are a lot of motherboards that use integrated RAM, and it is common for boards with onboard video to have integrated memory right next to the video chip. Even though it is integrated RAM used for the video chip it is also dedicated RAM in that it's only being used by the video chip. Without this integrated RAM, the video would have to share the RAM with the dedicated system RAM.

Slot Loaded RAM, the types, and how to insert or remove the sticks

This memory which is dedicated RAM, will lay flat, parallel to the motherboard. A desktop PC will use perpendicular slot loading, side by side. A laptop will either stack one atop the other, or side by side or one on either side of the board. Laptop memory rests in tab-locking ports. These ports have bent springy pins lined up in a row that will connect to the pins on the RAM stick – touching contact with both sides of the RAMs pins. Memory on a laptop will be inserted at a 45 degree angle pushing the RAM pin contacts into the motherboard DIMM ports insert slot. Once the pins are inserted and level, you will push the stick of ram flat to the motherboard and if aligned correctly will snap and lock into place. You should not have to struggle putting in RAM, if you are, you are doing it wrong and you need to start over removing and reseating.

Laptop RAM (random access memory) or Memory Types; Using only one slot, is it ok?

Using only one of the two (or more) slots available

Laptops are able to run using only one slot of the available 2. It appears there is a lot of controversy on this debate to which I don't know why. All laptops will run using only one stick of memory inserted, as long as it is the correct type for that model. It will also run if you insert the one stick into DIMM2 only as opposed to the main port DIMM1. Laptops that have integrated RAM and Dedicated RAM ports will run on only Integrated without having to install dedicated sticks.

Upgrading RAM

You can upgrade RAM in any laptop as long as it hasn't already been maxed out at its upgraded limits. All laptops will allow several different speed sequenced RAM types to be installed. Typically you will have 3 to 6 different choices of speed variances allowed for that chipset. If the wrong speed or an incompatible speed is installed, the system Boot Process will fault out and shut down the laptop.

Laptop Hard Drive Types and Compatibility (the 3 main types)

Laptop Hard Drive Types and Compatibility; Sata:

Serial ATA, Hard drive Specifications, Upgrading, Speeds

SATA connection will be a 2 slot connection, the 2 types common to laptops are slot or pin connection, unless an adapter is added, then ribbon and cable are used. The longer of the 2 slots is the Power connection, the smaller of the 2 is the Data connection slot. The 2 current, common speeds used in laptops are 4200 rpm, 5200 rpm (revolutions per minute) and 7200 rpm. If upgrading a hard drive, you will be able to also upgrade to a faster speed along with the size. With the added speed and size will come additional heat generated into the laptop during use, so keep this in mind when upgrading if your laptop already runs "hot", you will need to use additional cooling to dissipate the additional heat generated from upgrading. SATA allows for easy install, removal, and swapping due to its slot connection style, it also allows for greater speeds over PATA connection

Laptop Hard Drive Types and Compatibility; Pata-IDE

Parallel ATA, Hard Drive Specs, upgrading, speeds

This type of hard drive is identical to a SATA hard drive except for the connection. A PATA hard drive will have 2 rows of pins 40 pins in total. These Male pins will fit into the Female connection port on the motherboard. These hard drives will typically have an additional Jumper Pin section of 6 to 8 pins. You can add a 2 pin plastic jumper cap to a specific 2 pins to set the drive connection type such as Master, Slave or Cable Select. These hard drives were the common type before SATA came into the mix. They are now rarely used but are still around in all older laptops.

Laptop Hard Drive Types and Compatibility; SSD

Solid State Drive, Drive specifications, upgrading and speeds

The SSD cards are the newest (of the 3 discussed here) Media Mass Storage devices in use today. They are commonly found in the Netbooks, They are roughly 2 inches long by 1 inch wide, and resemble laptop Wi-Fi cards, and are virtually identical to them. They allow for compact manufacturing designs, and fan-less cooling. Currently the only downfall is the size limitations, which over time will expand. The other minor downside to these storage device choices is the chance for failure and permanent data loss from the failure. I have noticed that they can fail whether brand new or used for years, there is virtually no way to predict a failure and when it happens, your data is basically gone forever.

Laptop Cooling

Laptop Cooling; Fan and Heatsink functions and types:

The Heat sink Pipes and Radiator

The heat sink cools the laptop starting at the heat sink cooling contact plate. This plate is what rests above the component needing cooling, there can be more than one of these per heat sink and each separate plate will have its own pipe connected to it. The heat sink pipes will allow a route for the heat dissipating off the component or chipset to exit the laptop. The fan will help to pull the heat from the pipes and out through the radiator heat sink cooling fins which you will find on every laptop except for the fanless designs. The radiator is designed to extend the heat quickly throughout the thin metal plates that are aligned in a row very close together; the plates of the radiator will cool the air from the fan air passing through it sending a stream of cold air back up the heat sink pipe. All this will happen in a continuous motion pulling heat away while applying cold air to cool the component.

The reason for a heat sink and fan

The heat sink is needed to pull the heat from the components in the laptop. The fan will run thermally controlled, and will speed up or slow down according to the temperature increase or decrease. The heat sink and fan assembly will circulate air to and from the heating components, removing the heat and replacing with cool.

What components are the heat sinks cooling plates covering?

Heat sinks will cover the CPU or central processing unit; they will also cover the Southbridge chipset and the GPU or graphics chipset. Laptops will tent to integrate the Graphics and the Southbridge into one chipset to save space.

Fan-less Cooling Design

This is most prevalent in today's Netbooks, though is also currently being introduced into the high end laptop designs. The Rugged class of laptops will commonly use the fan-less design because of the necessity for sealed component enclosures. Fan-less design relies on the heat-spreader and unforced convection to dissipate heat. The heat-spreader is actually a thin metal shield underneath the keyboard, responsible for carrying heat away from the CPU, GMCH and ICH on the motherboard.

<u>Laptop Cooling;</u> **External/Internal cooling options**:

USB exhaust port fan

For the Best choice in Laptop Cooling, let me suggest the Mini Laptop USB Exhaust fan.

This little gadget is the best External cooling source option available to date for Laptops, Notebooks, and Netbooks alike. Reason being, a typical Laptop cooling pad is the type that is placed under the laptop, more commonly called a "laptop cooling pad". It usually consists of 2 or more fans that are supposed to "cool" the laptop.

These can and will work, though you need to consider a Few things when using one...

All Laptops Have A Cooling Cycle... They All Have Fan Input Ports... And they all have fan exhaust ports. But... Not all laptops have the Input Port for the CPU/GPU Fan on the Underside of the laptop... Some have it located on the Side or Rear... Then Have the Exhaust on Other Side Or Rear... If The Laptop Using the Sides and Not the Bottom/Underside has a Cooling Pad placed underneath... It Can Potentially hinder the Airflow Cycle, making it harder for the laptop to Cool in its Natural course... which is Proper Flow through the Exhaust port... And if you have a Fan on the Bottom Blowing Air up To the Bottom of the Laptop That has No Openings For Air Input, that Air Will Blow Up, then Spread To The Laptops Sides and not do much in the way of cooling the areas that need the heat dissipation. Though it can affect the internal airflow path and potentially slow it.

The Mini USB Exhaust Fan Gadget Connects right to the Laptops Existing Fan Exhaust Port Cage... It uses a Spring Loaded Universal Connector to allow it to connect to any size port cage area...

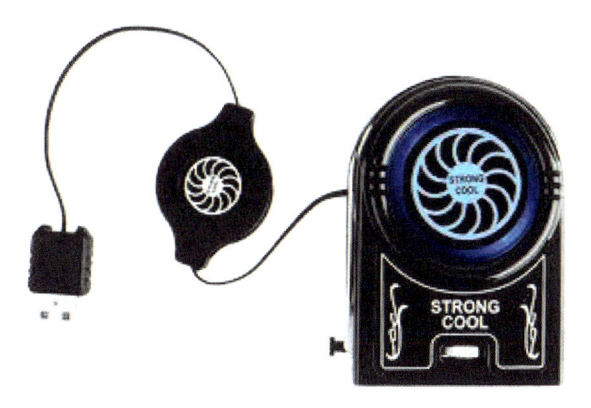

Then it has a retractable USB power cable built in so you can plug right into the laptop…

Also uses Blue LED Lighting to show Its Working/Spinning, and It has An Exhaust Port that Is Rotatable 360 degrees! The Function of the fan is to pull the Air from the Exhaust Port at a higher rate of speed than currently pulling… And allowing you to direct that air away in any direction needed… And actually helping a great deal in the cooling procedure.

Cooling pad, to use or not to use

Yes, they are good to use and can do a great deal for a laptop that tends to run hot or has a hard drive that overheats, though, you will need to refer to your laptops individual design to know if the cooling pad will benefit yours or hinder it. The average laptop base cooling pad will have fans that pull air/heat downward and then out the back end of the pad. This is good if the laptops input and exhaust ports are not in the cooling pad fans way. But if the fan on the laptop lines up with any of the cooling pad fans, it could potentially hinder the air flow and cause overheating issues or long term component failure.

Thermal paste usage and application

THE PROPER WAY TO APPLY THERMAL PASTE TO THE CPU (processor)

First off, let me stress the fact that you do not use Ceramic thermal paste (typically white) on a Laptop… You are to Only use Silver Thermal Paste (greyish-silver). The old paste must be removed from the CPU and from the heatsink before applying any new paste…

To remove any old paste, you can use a guitar pick to remove the crusty paste without scratching the surface of either part… Which you might overlook, but is very important… Even the slightest scratch can leave a "pit" which is going to also create a heat spot… where heat is concentrated on that area more than the flat level surface. So gently scrape off old, and follow up with wiping it using a paper towel piece. No Residue Liquid Flux is what I will typically use for chips that were initially loaded with paste from the factory and it has flowed over onto the components on the chips surface… It loosens the paste instantly for easy removal.

When you apply the new thermal paste, you are to use a Small amount. Do not glob it on, you want a paper thin layer, more importantly, you want a smooth and level surface. You do not just squirt on some paste and sit the heatsink on top… You take the paste and apply small dots, starting at a corner, then continue around to all corners. You then apply more dots throughout the chips surface, then, you will take a guitar pick or smooth plastic card and smooth out the paste, making it level.

Using copper shims on the heatsink

The Use of Copper Shims on the Graphics Chip

These Are To Only Be Placed On The Graphics Chip, And Not To The CPU… The CPU Gets a Silver Pad Or Silver Thermal Paste… If Using Shims (1 or 2) You Must As Well Use Silver Paste In Between the Shims

On the HP DV Series Laptops, I would recommend that you stick with using a thermal pad instead of using a shim…

And through further testing, using the original type thermal Pad on the GPU, and not a copper shim is a must on any hp dv series laptop motherboard…

There is a gap left between the chip and the heatsink on all DV series laptops (hp dv2000, dv6000, dv9000, TX series as well)

The use of a Pad ensures that there is sufficient heat dissipation from the chipset, and allows for the natural expansion and contraction of the chipset…

Use of a shim hinders this process and though initially it will appear to be helping, but it will eventually wear down the flip chip of the GPU by applying unneeded pressure to its surface.

Laptop Cooling; CPU **Fan Modification**:

How to make the fan run full speed all the time

MODDING THE CPU/GPU FAN

On certain model laptops, you can modify the fan to run at full speed all the time. Normally a Laptop is thermally controlled, and will speed up and slow down according to the internal temperature. On certain laptop models, this thermal controller is programmed too low, and the fan doesn't spin adequately enough to cool the GPU, which results in premature breakdown of the IC Chipsets BGA Connection, ending in Video Failure.

The Fans that are capable of Being Modified to Run Full Speed are the fans that use 4 wires, the fourth added wire being white in color. This wire is connected to the thermal controller component(s) on the motherboard and by disconnecting the white wire, you will bypass thermal control and the fan will free spin at full speed.

You will need to look closely at the fans wire plug end… the white plastic plug…

The white wire is held into the cap by a plastic locking tab strip… each wire going into the plug has one to secure it into the plug… use a razor blade or similar to raise the end of the tab upward to free the wire track. You can now pull the white out of the plug tip… Use needle nosed pliers, or I like to use my Mini flat head screwdriver to pull the white wire out. Bend it upward and tape it to the wires- away from the plug - using electrical tape or heat shrink wire tubing cover.

If you plug the fan back in and go to Power on the Laptop and NO Fan Spins at all… then you need to untape the wire and re-plug it into the cap, and Don't modify the fan, your laptop isn't accepting it… so don't mess with it.. In this case, you can try looking on the laptops Manufacturers Website … For Example, www.hp.com, for a BIOS update… and Install and Run it. It will most likely contain a fix for a slow CPU/GPU fan, to Speed up the thermal control, allowing the fan to run more often and speed up the fan, which is meant to prevent overheating and future GPU failure.

Fixing fan noise issues

A magnetic fan is the most commonly found in today's laptops, this fan type will run care free for the most part and will hold up to excessive dust and debris exposure. Though a fan can misalign and alter the way the fan spins, which could cause it to start hitting the housing of the fan or breaking a blade or deteriorating the magnet in the center of the fan. All this will cause noise coming from the fan, and when you first start hearing noise, you should be immediately investigating the issue. The most effective way to prevent fan noise is to regularly clean the fan and heat sink assembly. The fan will usually pull right away from the motor base for easy cleaning. Do not wet the fan and do not rinse it off, use a dry cleaning method for the fan, using a Q-Tip or toothbrush. If noise is already happening and cleaning does not help, you can try an electronics lubricant like WD-40 or similar to be applied to the fans center pin. This will allow the lubricant to clean both the pin and its female pin port which will hopefully release the excessive friction and quiet the fan.

Laptop Upgrading

Laptop Upgrading; Laptop Wireless Options (configuration and install):

How to install wireless if none exists

A lot of the older laptops had the capability to use wireless, though usually through the customer's needs at purchase it never was fully installed. You can check the screen and hinge area for Wi-Fi antennas or a singular one. Some laptops never ran the antennas up the screen and will be located somewhere in the casing of the laptop, which you will also need to locate. Then you will look for an empty Card port mini PCI port. If you have searched the entire laptop and motherboard, and no wireless is included, you will need to resort to a plug in style wireless option. This would include PC cards, USB devices, tethering and similar.

Adding internal antennas for Wi-Fi signal

If the laptop has a Wi-Fi card slot but no visible antenna(s), you can route you own antenna(s). I note singular antenna because some models would only use the main antenna wire for signal and not the auxiliary secondary wire. If you are installing a wireless card, you will be using 2 wire signal, the main and the auxiliary, or the white and black wires. If you have a wireless slot, you will most likely have tracks and slots for the antenna wires to travel up through the screen. You can purchase an antenna set from EBay, or you can pull a set from another machine. The ends of the antenna will have square or rectangular adhesive pads to which you will adhere these to the inside of the back screen cover. Typically the white or auxiliary wire will go on the right side of the panel housing and the black will go on the top left side. If you were to imagine splitting the back panel into 3 equal vertical sections, you would position the antenna adhesive ends on section one at the top and section 3 at the top, then you will run the wires around the sides of the display panel (there should already be tracks for the wires to set in. The wires will bend around the bottom of the display and down through the hinge area into the motherboard base area. You will need to ensure the wire countersink from any point on the palm rest area, if any portion is not, it will not allow the case to reassemble properly and you will have bumps in the case from the protruding wire. You will run the antennas all the way to the card, going through to the opposite side of the motherboard if needed. The most important thing to watch out for is preventing pinching of the wires, and ensuring the wires do not interfere with the case parts when reassembling.

Wireless card types, location of card port

The 2 most common are the mini-PCI and the mini-PCI express or mini-PCI-e. The main difference in the two is the size, the mini-PCI being double the size of the mini PCI-e card.

The Laptops Internal Parts and Components

The Laptops Internal Parts and Components; the Motherboard:

Differences between a Desktop PC motherboard and a Laptop motherboard

Size would be the biggest obvious difference, both the size of the PCB itself, and the size of the relative components attached.

Another big difference is the integration of the chipsets, like the GPU/Southbridge Merge, the Northbridge, GPU Merge, The GPU, Northbridge and CPU Merge, and the GPU, Southbridge, and CPU Merge. On a desktop motherboard, these will be typically be placed separate from one another.

The majority of capacitors on a Desktop motherboard will be electrolytic- tube style, while a laptops common capacitor is the ceramic capacitor, and will only have a few tube-style electrolytic Caps used, which is mainly due to space restrictions.

Expansion ports are different among the desktop and laptop, yet they exist in both versions. The laptops expansion ports and daughterboard ports will be small and will barely rise off the board, which is needed to be so, due to the lack of space. Because the connection port on the laptops motherboard won't protrude from the board very high, there will typically be securing screws to hold the part in place.

Colors of Motherboards, Icons on the motherboard, Part Identification

The two most common colors that laptop manufacturers use are blue and green. There are various different shades currently being used throughout the manufacturers, each trying to brand its own signature color for ease of recognition and reference.

Attached mini boards, daughter boards

It is hard to tell just by looking at your fully assembled laptop as to what parts and components are integrated or which are add on, or connected by a daughterboard or mini add on board. You would need to disassemble to visually inspect the inlay of that specific laptops internal components and parts.

Ability to use a compatible motherboard if an exact replacement is not available...

It is possible with certain models to replace with a compatible part, but you will need to physically inspect both the base of the laptop that it will be going into and the board itself. The main thing to look at is the motherboard and its setup. Look where all the components/ports etc… are located and you will need to compare to the existing motherboard to determine the similarities or differences. Sometimes to fit a compatible board you will be switching processor types, like, from AMD to Intel or possibly switching from a board that had integrated video to one that uses a dedicated card. If swapping boards and the CPU is altered from one make to a different make, be sure that the fan and heatsink assembly you are using in the swap out will properly fit, because chances are, you will need to also replace the fan assembly to fit the changed CPU. If swapping boards and the video differs, say from integrated to a card, you will most likely need to change the display cable to correctly fit onto the cards port, as it will be in a slightly different location on the board.

In some cases, you will need to slightly alter the bottom base where the motherboard is attached and secured to. I have found some compatible boards that will have one or 2 additional ports added that your original did not have. There is room in the base for these extra ports except that they were never cut out from the manufacturer. You will need to use a tool like a dremel (micro drill) to cut out the access port in the bottom base to properly fit the motherboard and allow the newly added ports to be functional and accessible.

The Laptops Internal Parts and Components;   DC Jack:

Plugging In, Preventing damage to the DC Jack and to the Adapter plug

When plugging in the AC Adapter, it is a good idea to ensure you are not twisting the cord, over time a twisted cable will get a "knot" or "bulge" which is actually the wires inside getting bunched up and weakening. If it continues to get twisted and untwisted in that same area, the internal protective wire coatings can deteriorate and cause the cord to short out. You should also try not to bend the cable near the tip area a lot, as it can greatly weaken the wires and can potentially cause faults in the tip itself. If you start needing to "wiggle" the cord to get positive power or to be able to charge the battery, it is a sign that the DC Jack is failing. It is best not to continue wiggling the cord tip in the Jack, as you can cause severe motherboard damage, especially if the jack pins are damaged.

Purpose of the DC Jack

The DC Jack is unique to each laptop or laptop series, and will use a unique plug tip for the AC Adapter, the DC stands for Direct Current, which is used to control Lower Voltages than AC Current. It also allows electricity to flow in one direction as opposed to bi-directional with AC current. The purpose of the DC jack is to provide quick access to the power source (the ac adapter).

Pin connection vs. Wire and Plug connection

The majority of laptops will use an onboard dc jack which is soldered directly onto the motherboard using pin and hole connections. This not only supplies the power (usually 12 volt, 5 volt and 3 volt, though these will vary per model), but also is what holds and secures the jack to the board.

The process of replacing the DC Jack

The process includes proper removal of the faulty DC Jack, not repair of the jack, as it is always best to replace the jack since they only cost $5.00(USD) per part on average. It is a small price to pay to not have to go back in a month just to re-repair the same jack that you didn't replace in the first place. The removal or desoldering process is discussed later in this book in the Desoldering section. It is next recommended that you remove the left over flux from the board when desoldering is completed. This is done either using circuit board cleaning solvents, or by scraping the flux off using a micro-sized flat-head screwdriver(make sure to scrape lightly to avoid scratching the motherboard and possibly breaking traces).

The next process is the soldering on of the new DC Jack, which is explained in detail in the Soldering section of this book. This process should take less time than the desoldering of the dc jack, and must be done correctly or you could ruin the motherboard.

With DC Jacks that are not located directly on the motherboard, you will have a choice to change the whole dc jack wire and plug set, or just the jack itself. Most of the time it will be easier to replace the whole jack/wire/ and plug set.

The Laptops Internal Parts and Components;   CD/DVD/Blu-ray Drives:

Proper cleaning of the Optical Lens

Optical drives will typically have the optical lens assembly located right in the slide out cd tray, and can be cleaned by simply ejecting the tray to gain access to the lens. You can use a professional quality lens cleaning kit, which will include a cleaning cd, a cleaning solution, and a cleaning cloth. With this kit, you will follow the directions on the package, which usually will want you to apply a small amount of solution to the cd and wipe clean with special cloth, then insert in cd tray and run for 60 seconds or so.

To manually clean the lens, you will use a cleaning solution and a cleaning cloth, adding a small amount of cleaning solution to the cloth and carefully and gently wiping the eye of the lens, then going over again with the dry area of the cloth to polish.

Slot loaded vs. Slide tray loading discs and drives

Slot loaded drives tend to be found in the higher end laptops and notebooks, and you will find them on most Macintosh/Apple laptops. There are good and bad points to using slot as opposed to slide out style. The good being that they are easier to use, just by placing the cd/dvd into the slot, the internal motor will pull the disc into the drive and start reading. There is less chance of part failure on the slot loaded drives due to it being mainly enclosed and all moving parts located internally. This helps to keep dust and debris out, and prevents damage to the holding tray. A slide tray drive can succumb to damage to the tray from constant use, and can become dislodged or break in the drive track area. These slide tray drives can also wear out due to the ability of dust and debris to enter both the tray area and the optical lens area, which over time can cause permanent damage.

I do not have many bad points about the drives except for the slot loading drives. Sometimes, when inserting and ejecting discs, they can become stuck in the drive. When this happens it is usually because the drive itself has become slightly misaligned from the slots opening port. It can get frustrating to get stuck discs out when this happens without having to disassemble and physically remove the stuck disc. You will typically have an eject key on the keyboard, or a certain button on the base of the laptop that you press or push to eject the disc. A lot of times when you have a stuck cd, these 2 eject options will not work to eject the disc, and unlike all slide tray drives that have an emergency eject access port/hole located on the tray, slot drives have no secondary eject access hole.   When a disc gets stuck, you should first try the keyboard or touch button to eject the disc, if that does not work, open My Computer and highlight the drives icon in that window, then choose Eject from the choices at the top of the window. If the disc still will not eject, you can apply slight pressure to the area on the palmrest at the edge of the laptop right above the slots disc port, then press the eject key or button simultaneously. Switch to the bottom side if the upper side did not work, then, if none of these options ejected the disc, you will need to disassemble the laptop to gain access to the internal drive, then realign the drive housing until it will properly accept and eject discs smoothly.

The Laptops Internal Parts and Components;   Floppy Drives:

External floppy drives, internal drives and their use today

Floppy drives are not used anymore, but can still be found on most of the older laptops. Back when they were popular, the technology had not yet evolved to allow for larger data/media capacity storage. Even as CD drives were starting to be used, people still used the floppy for the storing of smaller amounts of data, such as text or document style files, which didn't take up much space per file. When DVDs and Blu-Ray came into use and popularity, the floppy drive died out and was no longer used in laptops. You still are able to use floppy discs by purchasing a compact external floppy drive enclosure that plugs into the laptop via USB slot. These are readily available and are relatively low cost.

The Laptops Internal Parts and Components; SD Card / Slot Cards:

Usages and location on the laptop

SD cards will most commonly be the camera style cards. You will have a slot located on the front or side(s) of the laptop to insert the card. It will lock in place by pushing it all the way in, then to release the card you will again push the car in, then let go and it will spring out of the slot enough for you to grab ahold and remove. The SD cards are constantly changing in the amount of allowable storage space, and you can have the ability to use that card as "virtual" memory for your laptop if your Laptop gives you that option (found in Vista and Windows 7). The memory program is usually called "ready boost" and will turn your storage SD card into Memory or RAM, and will use this RAM if needed to keep things running at full speed.

Different types of SD and Slot Loading Cards and Peripherals

You will find a PCMCIA slot on the side of your laptop, which allows for a credit card sized device to connect like plugging in a USB device. The most common use for this slot is to add a Wireless card to the laptop. You can also find multiple uses and devices that use this slot from Ethernet ports to USB ports to external sound cards. They are still common and will be found in most laptops manufactured today.

Flash Memory Card Reader/Writers and Memory Types - a laptops memory card readers and writers are used to transfer files such as digital pictures, mp3s, data files, and PDA files between computer and Memory Cards

CF Compact Flash - Small and durable.

Microdrive IBM Microdrive - Super Fast, allows up to 1GB capacity, the same size as CF.

SD Secure Digital - Same size as MMC cards with encryption capabilities.

SM Smart Media - Very small and thin.

MMC MultiMedia Card - Small with high transfer speeds, more durable.

MS Memory Stick - Same standard used by Sony

xD xD-Picture Card - New and Small Flash technology developed by Fuji

Setting up Ready-Boost on the SD card

To set up Ready Boost, you will be editing the Removable Disk Properties. Usually when you first insert your SD card, you will get a pop up window taking you directly to the properties window and right to the Ready Boost Tab to edit the settings and enable it. You will also have a slider bar to use as much of that card as memory as you like, you can use all of it, or just a portion. The other way to access these settings would be to go to My Computer, highlight the SD card Icon and choose "properties" from the drop-down list.

Laptop Issues

Laptop Issues;   Non-Powering On Issues:

Process of elimination testing procedures

Testing All Motherboards Is a Process of Elimination...Ruling out one thing... going to the next in line possibility...

First thing to check is the AC Adapter (the charger)...Use a multimeter for this, put the black negative prod on the outside of the plug tip, and put the red positive prod on the inside of the plug tip...

Next check the DC Jack

There are 2 general types of DC Jacks... Onboard.... and Off board/Extended

The onboard dc jacks, the ones that are directly soldered to the motherboard are typically the ones that fail. The Off board or the ones that use a wire connection and rest in a slot in the case... Are 100 times more stable... because they are able to move slightly if needed when over-torque is applied....

You need to visually inspect the pins on the DC Jack from both sides of the motherboard... If the Jack is faulty, you can usually see the melted solder/missing solder/burn-out spot/short...If the Jack and Pin Connections Look Good then it's time to test with multimeter... You need to test the pin area, and surrounding ceramic capacitors/Fuses.

DC Jack Is Good, What Next?

Next you need to make absolutely sure all Hardware is functioning properly...

Test The Hard Drive, Test Your RAM, and Test Your CPU (though this is typically not the issue)

Determining the cause (software or hardware related)

Testing a non- powering on laptop by listening for any high pitched buzzing noises. To do this... you need to separate yourself from any surrounding noise... like turning off any fans, TVs, Radios... etc...

You need to Physically inspect the motherboard, using a lighted magnifying glass, you can find an exact replacement for the blown capacitor by removing one from a dead motherboard... otherwise you will need to buy some capacitors.. (not an easy find)..

Symptoms of a Blown capacitor.... When you plug in the AC Adapter, and the green power light on the adapter goes out... Resulting in No Power to the laptop...

If you find a Blown Capacitor, You need to Replace it... You Desolder it from the motherboard .. You must be extremely careful in doing so, because if you overheat the contact pads that the capacitor connects to, you won't be able to resolder a new cap onto the motherboard...

Add a Tiny amount of Flux paste to each end of the Cap, then use a thin desoldering braid (solder wick) and touch the end of the Cap with it, take your soldering gun and touch it to the desoldering braid - then touching the capacitor end to remove the thin layer of solder covering it... you don't need to remove all the solder.... Do this once again to the opposite end....

Now you use a Micro-Sized Flat Head Screwdriver and gently touch the side of the capacitor (you will be pushing on the Cap to remove it), Touch your soldering guns tip to the end of the Capacitor, and at the same time, gently apply pressure with the screwdriver to the side of the Cap to push it sideways off it's Pad..Heat the End to melting point ... then Quickly switch to the opposite end and heat... the capacitor will "Pop" Off and Roll Off it's Pad. Now you can Solder a New One On...

NOTE: I use a Black Permanent Marker When Removing a Capacitor... Color the TOP of the Capacitor All Black.. this way, when you remove the capacitor - you will know which side is the top...

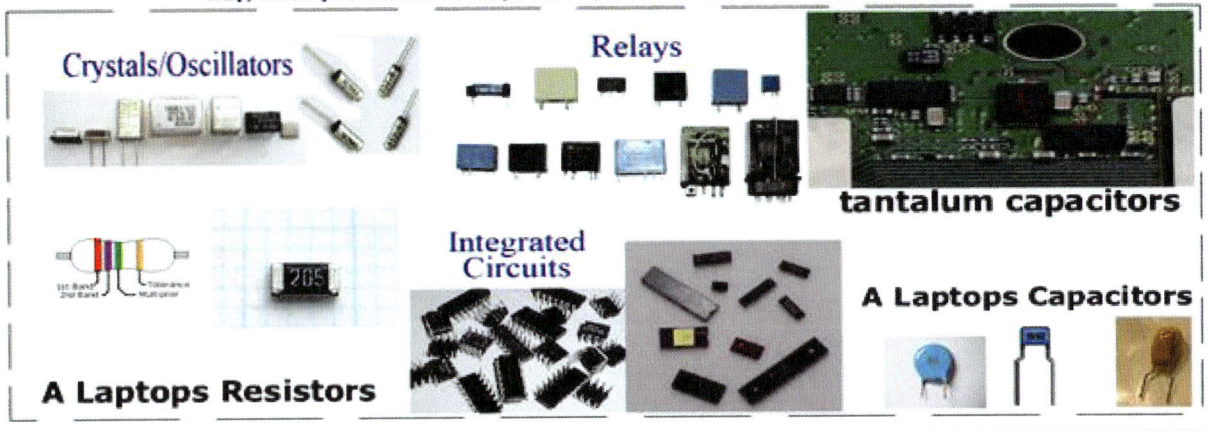

Plug in the AC Adapter into the DC Jack and press the Power Button on the Motherboard (whether the board is in the casing or not doesn't matter), then hold your ear up to the laptop or motherboard and move your head around to listen for any noises coming from blown components... Do not worry, the motherboard Won't shock you...as it is self-grounded.

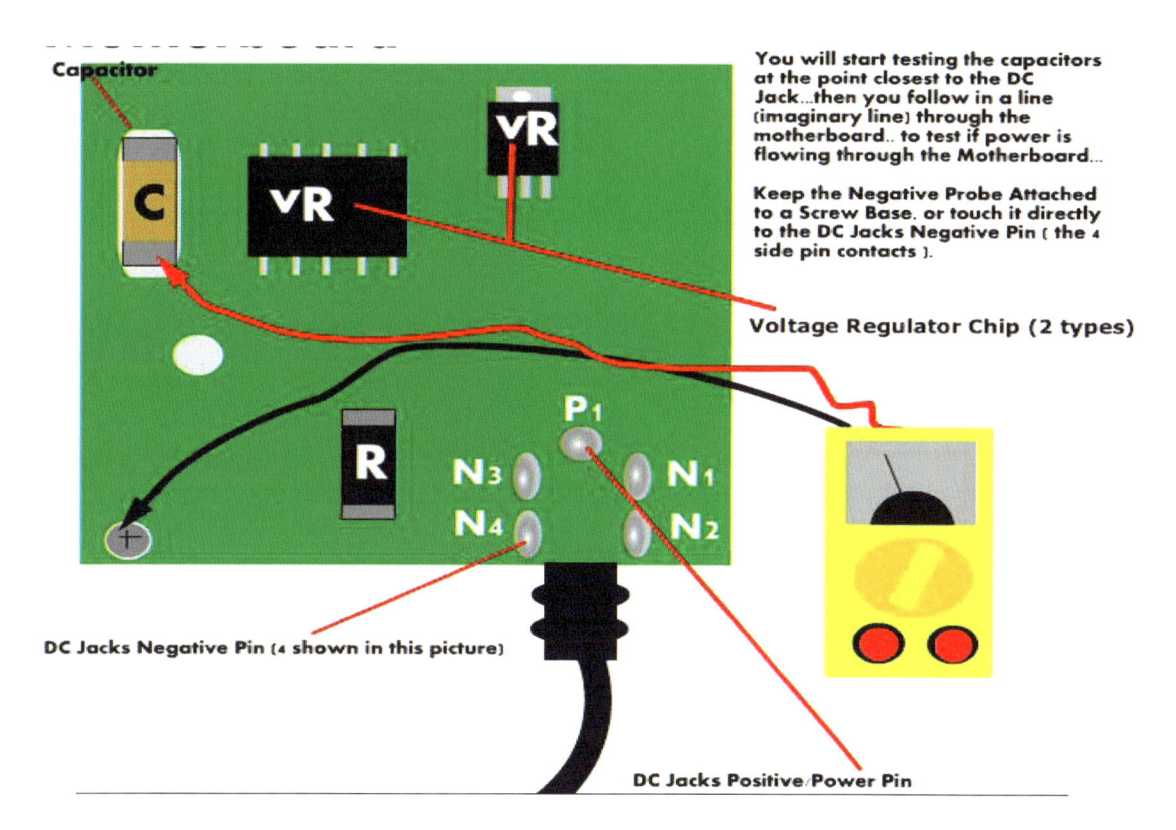

Capacitor

C

vR

vR

R

N3 **N1**
N4 **N2**

P1

You will start testing the capacitors at the point closest to the DC Jack...then you follow in a line (imaginary line) through the motherboard.. to test if power is flowing through the Motherboard...

Keep the Negative Probe Attached to a Screw Base, or touch it directly to the DC Jacks Negative Pin (the 4 side pin contacts).

Voltage Regulator Chip (2 types)

DC Jacks Negative Pin (4 shown in this picture)

DC Jacks Positive/Power Pin

Check the DC Jack and AC Adapter Next, You can check the dc jack to AC adapter connection sometimes by simply plugging in the cable and gently wiggling the plug into the port area, and if you get and lose power when this is done, you are closer to determining that the DC Jack is faulty. Disassembly will then be needed to test further, and visually inspect the jack.

Misseated RAM Sticks can also cause the laptop to not Power on/boot up. You should remove the RAM sticks and reseat them... If Still No change, you can try adding one stick at a time then attempting to power on. Next you need to test the AC Adapter for positive Power reaching the tip...

Testing the AC Adapter can be done a couple ways... If you have an exact replacement Adapter that is known to be "working", Then by all means, Try Using that cord to see if you get the same results...If not, you will need to use a multimeter to test power to the plug tip.. You would touch the Negative prod to the outer side of the plug tip and place the positive (red) prod inside the ac adapter plug tip end. Set the multimeter to test voltage/ or set it to beep upon positive power connection to test.

Visual inspection can and should also be done to the tip area of the adapter... If the tip has Knots and bends in the cord area near the tip, that might be an indication that there is a short. You can also grab the plastic plug end and also grab the metal tip end and slightly and gently wiggle the metal tip portion back and forth with the tip held up to your ear... if you hear a Clicking sound.. it is most likely that the tip itself has a broken connection..

A Faulty CPU can sometimes cause the laptop not to power on, though in this case, it will usually power on and immediately shut down, not to mention, the CPU is one of the most stable components inside the laptop, as it doesn't typically overheat, and if overheating is to occur, it will usually affect the GPU before affecting the CPU. So this would be a last resort test, which would be to disassemble and swap out the CPU to ensure it is not the fault.

A faulty video chip/GPU BGA (ball grid array) connection could also cause non powering on issues.. And a reflow would be needed to test. You can first test the laptop by connecting an external monitor to the laptop to see if an image displays on it... If Not, then this brings you closer to determining that it is in fact a video issue, And Disassembly would be needed along with a chip reflow to determine if the video is the fault.

Assuming you have already tested and ensured that your power cord is working correctly... Look for broken Pin connections, Look for burn spots, Look for the solder melted away from the Jacks Center pin(s), and you should also test the Power on the motherboard to ensure that the power is flowing through the DC Jack and into the Motherboard. Do this by connecting the Negative Probe of a multimeter (set it to view DC) to the negative Pin on the dc jack... This will be one of the Side pins on the jack...then touch the positive probe of the multimeter to the center back pin of the dc jack and look at the multimeter to see of power is flowing into the motherboard.

Double and Triple check to ensure you have properly diagnosed the issue at hand.

Laptop Issues;   **Overheating Issues:**

Random shut downs and the reason why

Laptops are thermally controlled and will spin the fan blade(s) when the sensors tell it to do so. The fan will run slower when needed and will speed up when needed and will idle when told to do so. A lot of the laptops will have BIOS updates released that when installed, will speed up the fan and allow it to run at loner intervals to keep the components cooler than previous. The most common reason for laptop failure is Overheating. The usual way the laptop will overheat is due mainly to poor design. Every laptop needs to be cleaned to ensure clear and proper air flow and this hold true for both laptop and desktop computers. The air exhausting from the laptop passes through the heatsink radiator fins. The lint, dust and debris will also exhaust through this route and will eventually collect on the face of the radiator fins. Eventually, blockage will occur and a lint trap will form. It will resemble the lint build up that a Home dryer will get, where you need to "peel" the lint from the trap and reinsert it into the dryer, the same applies for the laptop. The lint trap build up will need to be removed from the heatsink, then the dust between the fins will need to be blown out.

When Overheating occurs, the Sensors are programmed to shut down the laptop to prevent further damage to the internal components on the motherboard. You will typically see a blue screen if powered on and the operating system is running. You can also view your registry's Event Viewer history reports to see if indeed Heat was the cause.

A laptop that is shutting down at different times, and not at a certain point every time, will usually indicate that it is an overheating issue.

If you were to take the heatsink off of the CPU and GPU, then unplug and remove the fan, then power on the laptop, it would run for around 5 to 10 seconds and then shut down. Every laptop will shut down when overheated. If it continued to run and run, it would blow out the GPU first and then the CPU.

The importance of a proper cleaning on a regular basis

On average, it will take about 6 months to get to the point where the laptop will need to have its fan and heatsink cleaned. The longer a laptop runs with a clogged heatsink the more irreversible damage will occur to its components. It will weaken and strain the components by making them work harder and run at temperatures they were not designed to run optimally at. The heat can cause deterioration in the material itself of that individual component. It can also weaken the solder joint connections to the components causing long term failure.

Fixing overheating issues and different methods used

1. Cleaning the heatsink and fan assembly is the first thing to do
2. Applying new thermal paste or a thermal pad is also done
3. Copper shim use is becoming common, but must be done correctly or the reverse effects will occur.
4. Fan modification can be done to run the fan at full speed
5. External cooling such as Laptop Cooling Pads can be used

Laptop Issues;   Non Booting Issues:

Determining the cause, process of elimination testing

COMMON NON BOOTING ISSUES AND PROCESS OF ELIMINATION TESTING PROCEDURES

First and easiest thing to check is the Memory. You will find the memory located on the bottom side of the laptop, though some models to put the Memory under the keyboard area as well.

Mis-seated Memory or Incorrect Speed Memory or The Wrong Density/Velocity Memory can all Cause this to occur. Certain Failing Hard Drives Can Also Cause this to happen. A failing or Faulty Video Card or Chip can also Cause this as can a Failing Rechargeable Battery…

The first thing to do when this is happening is to check for proper voltage at the end of your AC Adapter (charging cord), A short in the wire can reverse power and cause the laptop to shut down. Or an incorrect AC Adapter can as well cause this to occur.

A Blown Voltage Regulator Chip, Or Any other component such as a ceramic capacitor, or fuse That has blown, can cause the laptop to Attempt to Power on then immediately Shut down..

A Faulty Video Chip or card Will cause the laptop to shut off when attempting to Power on, this is due to the Laptop not passing POST, the Chipset is not recognized as existing/or has been recognized as Faulty and it Shuts Down.

Assuming you have already tested and ensured that your power cord is working correctly…

You will first, remove the battery, then once again, test powering on using AC Adapter alone… Still No Power, You will need to check the DC Jack. The DC Jack is the port where you plug the charger cable into on your Laptop.

Look for broken Pin connections, Look for burn spots, Look for the solder melted away from the Jacks Center pin(s), and you should also test the Power on the motherboard to ensure that the power is flowing through the DC Jack and into the Motherboard. Do this by connecting the Negative Probe of a multimeter (set it to view DC) to the negative Pin on the dc jack… This will be one of the Side pins on the jack…then touch the positive probe of the multimeter to the center back pin of the dc jack and look at the multimeter to see of power is flowing into the motherboard. A Bad DIMM slot or Misseated Hard Drive Can, On Rare Occasion Cause This Too.

Now, if the repair in question is not your personal laptop and you do not know the history of that laptop… meaning if you do not know firsthand exactly how the laptop was running before the power on/boot up failure, you will need to find out if the owner attempted a BIOS update and the issue is because of a BIOS update that went wrong… This will be an uncommon reason for the non-working laptop, yet it needs mentioning because it most certainly is a possibility.

If someone attempted to do a BIOS update and it quit the install Mid-Way… or somehow did not complete the update… the laptop / motherboard can be left non-working… Meaning … it will usually power on… but all you will get is a blank screen … or sometimes a blinking cursor… In this case, you will need to have the BIOS re-flashed, or swapped if allowable.

If No Testing that you are doing seems to be giving you any clear answers as to what is wrong, you will now be fully disassembling the laptop in question to start by testing the motherboard alone…

Once fully disassembled, you will have only the motherboard in front of you. Add the Ram to the motherboard, keep the Cmos battery plugged in if you have the plug in type… and add the CPU, heatsink and fan assembly. If able to, connect an external monitor to the VGA/DVI port, and plug the hard drive into the port.

Attempt to Power On… And Both Look And Listen to the Motherboard and All the Components. Listen for any buzzing or beeping, and look for any dark spots, blown capacitors or any other components. Also you will be watching the External Monitor for power on and Video POST…Please note here that if you do not have an external monitor to connect to the laptop, you can plug the display cable from the laptops screen into the motherboard… Making sure that if that laptop has a separate inverter cable wire, you plug that in as well.

If the motherboard powers on, then immediately powers back off… you should check the DC Jack, the CPU, the GPU, the RAM, The Hard Drive, and possible blown component(s).

If the motherboard powers on then shuts off, then powers back on and off in cycle… you should check the CPU, the GPU, the RAM, and the Motherboard for blown components or a Short, or Possible liquid damage to the board.

If the motherboard powers on then continues to run but no display and no light to the screen, you should check the GPU for BGA failure, Reseat the RAM or test with replacement RAM, and check the motherboard once again.

If the motherboard powers on and can display video, yet shows NO hard drive installed in the BIOS (when in fact there is one connected, and known to be working properly), you should check the motherboard, mainly the hard drive controller IC chip…which, you will need to view the motherboard schematics sheet to locate. Another thing to try if this happens is a BIOS update … and this would have to be done by a USB installed Flash update.

If the laptop powers on, has video, recognizes hard drive, yet will not install the operating system, or any operating system, you will need to first check BIOS setup Utility to see if in fact the Hard Drive is recognized, then, if it is, try 2nd or 3rd different CD/DVD of the Operating System if available. Some laptops will not install certain versions of Windows CD Installs due to the CD not having integrated SATA drivers to recognize the SATA hard drive… In this case … you would need to integrate that SATA driver for your laptop model into the CD-ROM… there are instructions available on the WEB to do that… Google It... Then of course, you will need to test the hard drive for potential failure/head crash/bad sectors-clusters etc…

Laptop Powering On But Has Blank-Black Screen

The first thing you need to do is to hold the screen up to a bright light... Looking to see if you have a working Display and just might have a blown power inverter or Bulb... If No Video is visible and you are pretty sure that it is a Black-blank screen… you will now connect an external monitor to the laptop to check if you are able to view anything on it… If No External Video As Well... you most likely have a Video Failure Issue... though it can be other things… Video is typically the culprit. Reflowing the GPU will be needed if determined the Video Chip is at fault.

Another Thing That Causes This Issue Is a Corrupted BIOS, if you were in the middle of a BIOS Flash or Update, and somehow the BIOS update did not complete successfully, You Could Be Stuck with NO BIOS, Which Would Produce A Blank Screen in Some Cases…

Here you would check the Ram too, If misseated or the wrong type, it will produce blank screen issues.

Check the CPU, if it is not locked down, it will do the same thing, Blank-Black screen... This will also cause shut down on some machines...

On rare occasion, Board Flex... will cause this to happen...Board Flex Happens to a motherboard a lot of ways… It can happen to a laptop that has weak parts, like thin-bendable plastic used for the palmrest and bottom base, or models like the IBM ThinkPad, a bad case design that leaves no middle support and the board is flexed when picked up from the front over and over…What it does is it creates cracks and faults in the traces through the motherboard... these are not repairable and the Motherboard will for sure need to be replaced to correct the issue.

Laptop Powers On, Then Immediately Shuts Down

Common Causes Are:

The CPU – Either the wrong type or failure has occurred

Bad RAM – or Misseated Ram causes this issue

Overheating causes this (a blocked heatsink radiator)...

Sometimes, A Bad Hard Drive can cause this... I have not yet come to a conclusion as to why this happens to certain hard drives ... but I have experienced it first hand and know it is a possibility.

A plugged in USB Device can sometimes cause this issue... so check all ports and remove all USB Connected devices to test...

Blown fuses/Capacitors and so forth on the motherboard will also cause the laptop to do this... and a complete motherboard inspection will be needed to determine if it is causing the issue.

Once again, Liquid Damage to the motherboard or any part or component will show signs of this issue... So Check these things first, as they are the most common causes of the laptop powering on and immediately shutting itself back off...

Laptop Issues;   **CD-DVD Drive not working / not recognized:**

Deleting the upper and lower filters from the registry

Click on Start (lower left corner of the laptop screen), Run, and type REGEDIT and press Enter. Look for the Folder labeled: HKEY_LOCAL_MACHINE, then in the sub category window, choose: SYSTEM; then choose: Current Control Set; then: Control; then: Class; then select the yellow folder labeled: {4D36E965-E325-11CE-BFC1-08002BE10318}

This folder is the DVD/CD-ROM Drive Class Description in the registry. Look for any of the following names in the right hand column:

* UpperFilters

* LowerFilters

* UpperFilters.bak

* LowerFilters.bak

If any of the above keys are listed, right-click on them and choose Delete. After deleting the keys, close the Registry Editor and reboot your laptop. Upon boot up, open My Computer and check to see if your CD or DVD drives have returned.

Laptop Screen / Video Issues

Laptop Screen / Video Issues; No video on the laptops screen:

Connecting an external screen or monitor for testing purposes

All laptops will have a VGA, DVI, HDMI, or S-Video out port on it to send the video to an outside source. The most common is the VGA, which you can plug a Desktop PCs monitor into. Plug in the monitor, and power on the laptop, by default, the external monitor will power on if video is working.

Determining if it is a video issue or if it is screen problems

It is easiest to first rule out the possibility of video failure by connecting an external monitor. If you can produce video to the external source, you can rule out potential video problems and concentrate on looking into the Screen as the cause of the failure. For testing the screen, start with a visual inspection, then check the power inverter, the display cable and then finally checking the display panel itself for failure.

Laptop Screen / Video Issues; Lines on the screen:

Start by checking the display cable, here's how…

You will need to remove the display cable from the laptop, and to do so, you will first need to disassemble the screen to get to the upper connection port located on the rear side of the screen. Once you have the upper half of the display cable separated, you should reconnect the cable into its plug to then power on and test if reseating the upper connection fixed the issue. If not, unplug the cable once again and continue to disassemble the lower base parts to reveal the lower port connection on the laptops motherboard. Unplug the cable from the motherboard and inspect both the plug end and the motherboard port for damage like bent pins or blocked holes. You will then re-plug the cable into the bottom port and test by powering on the laptop. If still not fixed, you will keep the cable connected and power on the laptop, gently wiggle and bend the cable with the display being powered on, keeping an eye on the screen to see if your image comes back when the cable is bent. It will then need to be physically inspected for any breaks or knots in the cable.

Determining if there is damage to the screens rear circuit board panel

Laptop manufacturers are continuing to look for ways to lighten the total weight of the laptops they make, and in doing so, the Laptop itself can be a lot more fragile than the laptops built 5 to 10 years ago. The plastics used are lighter, less metals are being used for bracing and support, instead lighter and stronger plastics are being integrated. The screens on a lot of laptops are becoming thinner and thinner, and along with the thinness will come the chance for screen flexing issues to occur. Screen flexing can easily happen on a laptop with inadequate support, and can cause damage to both the display and to the displays rear circuit board or controller board. Opening and closing the laptops lid can take a lot of torque and can create a lot of applied pressure to one side of the screen more than the other side at one time, which will cause the screen and its internal parts to bend and flex. Over time this can cause damage to the circuit board by blowing components, breaking traces, or knocking components right off the panel. You can tell if this issue is what you are facing by gently flexing the screen back and forth. You will grab ahold of both sides of the upper screen corners, pulling on one side and pushing on the opposite, then alternating back and forth (slightly). If you can fix the issue by re-flexing the screen, you can determining that the screen you are working on has suffered this flex issue. You will need to replace the screen to fix the issue unless you are able to temporarily repair it with rubber pressure pads. In most cases, it will only worsen and you will only be prolonging the inevitable repair to come.

Temporary repair to remedy the line issue

Once you have determined that screen flex has occurred, you can narrow down the area of fault by switching the position of your hands and flexing the screen in different areas along the top of the screen. Once the location where you can get the screen to show correctly has been determined, you can take a thick rubber pad, like the ones that are used as "shoes" or "feet" on the bottom of the laptop, and position it affixed to the rear upper rail of the display panel. Re-secure the display panel to its metal side rails and reassemble the screen. Power on the laptop and test to see if the display repair holds up and no more lines are present by opening and closing the lid numerous times to test the flex issue.

Laptop Screen / Video Issues;   **Faint image but no backlight:**

Process of elimination testing to determine the fault

This can be only a couple different things…

Either the CCFL bulb (LCD) has Blown, or the Power inverter Board is the fault…

Sometimes the display cable will cause this, and it would be due to a fracture in the cable wires, or the cable being crimped in the hinge area, or similar…. But Most of the time it is the Bulb or The Inverter that has caused this issue to occur.

Determining If Your LCD Bulb Has Failed

A failing bulb will sometimes give off clues that it's failing… It will flash on and off, it will sometimes give off soft colors too, like pinks and greens and reds (not dark color, Light faded Color…)

Look to see if you can see the display running in the screen with no light…If you have no light to the display, it is typically only one of 2 things that would be at fault… The Inverter or the Bulb…

Replacing the Bulb is Not a difficult task though it does take a lot of patience...You will need to remove any screws along the sides of the screen, then look at each side right and left where the circuit board ends on both sides, remove screws ..

you will need to carefully cut the plastic tape along the metal screen frames edge to release the frame, then pull the frame away from the screen pulling it from its tabs...

Then remove the tin backing that helps lock the screen together, then, you will carefully remove the bulb...

To replace the bulb you can do a couple things... If you do regular screen repairing, you will have a lot of broken screens lying around... You can use the bulbs from the broken screens so long as they still light up when connected.. Or you can get a replacement bulb ordered from the internet, or EBAY... But be for-warned... when ordering one off the internet or EBAY, it will typically be the bulb only... and it will not have the 2 wires or the plug connected to it... just a basic bulb with a wire posts on either end. You will need to solder new wires and a plug tip to the bulb... you can as well buy these on EBAY when available, make sure you buy the correct length/size in correspondence to your bulb.

To Remove the LCD Bulb, you first will flip the screen over to its back side... the top side will be where the circuit panel is located... Look for a micro sized screw on both sides of that panel that secure it to the screens back side... Unscrew and remove these (2)... then turn the screen on the side and look for the same sized screws on the sides of the screen... On many models, there will be 2 or more... Remove all...

Then you will need a razor blade to cut around the parameter of the screen.. Meaning, there are many stickers that wrap from the sides/top onto the back side... and you need to cut along the point where the front metal frame cover meets the under metal screen frame... Which means you run the blade along the entire top side of the back of the screen, then there will be areas on both sides that need cutting... be careful here and make a shallow cut not a deep one...

Now you will be able to pry the front metal frame from the screen, start pulling from the top corner.. it is secured to the screen using metal Bump tabs.. You use a thin plastic tool or your micro size flat head screwdriver to "pop" the frame loose from the screen... Pull it downward away from the front of the screen but don't completely remove it... you can leave it attached at the bottom.

 You will have to gently pull the white plastic front bracing frame away from the bulb, then at the same time, you will pull up on the inner metal bulb housing... pulling it in an upward motion and starting from either the left or the right side...before pulling the bulb and bulb housing away from the screen, you will need to De-Route the LCD Bulb wires... Start at the point where they come out of the screen, Pull them one at a time through the opening in the slot holder, then unstick them from the plastic so that the wires are free from the screen...

Now Remove the LCD Bulb and Replace..

Power Inverter Board

This part will fail and the laptop will not get backlighting... And typically the transformer in the board is what fails... If you have an inverter with a similar transformer, you can solder it in place of the faulty one to revive the inverter. If that doesn't fix it, you can test the ceramic capacitors and the fuse(s) to hopefully find a fault... Otherwise it is simply easier to just replace with a new inverter... All models are available on EBAY... And will cost around $10-$20 USD. To Test the Inverter, an easy way is to attach a different LCD Bulb to it... I usually Attach the bulb from a broken screen (one that lights up, I use these because I already know it has a known working bulb in it)... And if it will light up... the inverter is good... if it will not light the bulb... the inverter needs repairing or replacing...You can as well connect a multimeter to the inverter plug end, and try to get a reading for power or no power..

But again... the easiest thing to do is to simply replace the power inverter as they are relatively cheap and readily available.

Power Issues

Power Issues;   No Power at All:

Troubleshooting and process of elimination testing procedure

The first thing to check:

Listening to the Motherboard

Another Great Laptop Testing Tool is your Ear....

Testing a non- powering on laptop by listening for any high pitched buzzing noises. To do this... you need to separate yourself from any surrounding noise... like turning off any fans, TVs, Radios... etc...

Plug in the AC Adapter into the DC Jack and press the Power Button on the Motherboard (whether the board is in the casing or not doesn't matter), then hold your ear up to the laptop or motherboard and move your head around to listen for any noises coming from blown components... Do not worry; the motherboard won't shock you...as it is self-grounded.

Continuity or short circuit test

Continuity checks ensure a reliable, low resistance connection between two points. For example, check the continuity of a cable between two connectors to ensure that both ends are connected properly. Set your analog multimeter to a low resistance scale (X1 Ohms), short (touch) the red and the black probes together, the pointer will go to zero ohm. If it is not zero, adjust the zero adjuster for bringing the pointer to exact zero ohms. Now, connect the two probes to the points where the short or continuity is to be checked, If the meter shows zero Ohm, it means the continuity is present or the connection internally not broken. Ideally, a good continuity should be about 0 Ohm.

You can also use a digital meter that have the buzzer sound to test the connection. If you heard the buzzer sound while measuring the wire or connection, this means that the connection or internal wire is good.

Resistance and Resistors

The main two characteristic of resistor are its resistance R in ohms and its power rating in watts, W. Resistors are available in a very wide range of R values from a fraction of an ohm to many mega ohms. The power rating may be as high as several hundred watts or as low as 1/8 watt. Always use a replacement resistor with a power rating that is equal to or greater than the original. The value of the resistance can be measure by a multimeter.

Types of Resistors

Carbon-Composition Resistors

Carbon-Film Resistors

Metal-Film Resistors

Wire Wounds

Fusible Resistor

Variable Resistor

There are two ways of testing resistor; using an analogue or digital multimeter. Normally if a resistor fails they will either increase in value or open up at all (open circuit). You can check the resistor resistance by selecting the ohmmeter range in the analogue and digital multimeter. If the resistor is in circuit, you will generally have to remove the resistor so you are testing only the resistor value and not the other components in the circuit. Always be aware of possible back (parallel circuit) circuits when checking in-circuit resistance measurements.

Measuring a fuse on board with a digital or analog multimeter

Touch the probes to both end of the fuse. You can check the fuse while it still in circuit. A good fuse reading should showed continuity or read ZERO ohms. A blown fuse is open which will not show any reading on your meter. You may also set to the buzzer range to test a fuse with digital meter. If the fuse is ok, the buzzer will sound and if the fuse is broken (internally) there will be no sound. Testing fuse is one of the simplest tasks in electronic troubleshooting-it is easy and fast. For fuse replacement, use only the same current and voltage ratings as the original one.

Testing Coil/Inductors

Testing a coil is very easy compares to checking three leads components such as SCR, FET and etc. In general, a coil consists of many turns or wire wrapped around a common core. The core could be made of iron or even air. It is label as "L" on circuit board. When an electric current passes through the coil, a magnetic field is produced. A coil in some respects acts just opposite a capacitor. A capacitor blocks DC while allowing AC to flow through it; a coil allows DC to flow through it while restricting AC current flow. Another name for a coil is an inductor.

Testing Diodes

Set your analog meter to x1 ohms range to check for current diode leakage reverse and forward testing. Connecting the red probe of your meter to the cathode and black probe to the anode, the diode is forward biased and the meter should read some value of resistance. Touch the black probe of your meter to the cathode and red probe to the anode, the diode is reverse biased and should look like an open reading-the meter pointer not moving. If you get two readings then most probably the diode is shorted or leaky and you should replace it. Always replace a diode with the same or higher rating than the original specification.

Testing electrolytic capacitor with digital capacitance meter

Connect the test probe to the capacitor and read the results from the meter LCD display. Example: a 100 microfarad should have the reading of somewhere 90 microfarad to 120 microfarad. Remember, capacitors have tolerance just like resistors. Be sure to discharge the capacitor first before testing. A reading of 60 microfarad means the capacitor has lost its capacitance and need to be replaced. This meter is more expensive than analogue meter. Somehow digital capacitance meter have their own disadvantage, which is, it can't check a capacitor that is breaking down when under load and it can't check capacitors in circuit. It's still worth to invest in this meter because it can check almost 80-90 % of capacitors failure.

ESR Meter Testing

The third and most accurate method is to use an ESR meter which stand for equivalent series resistance. This is the latest technology in testing capacitors. It can only check electrolytic capacitors and the advantage is that you can perform capacitor testing while the capacitor is still in circuit and have the accuracy of 99% compare to other meters. It is fast and can discharge a capacitor before it begin to test the capacitor and save you a lot of time. ESR meters are the most reliable and accurate meter for testing Caps.

Testing Ceramic Capacitors

The ceramic capacitor leakage quite often happened when there is a high voltage applied into it. Under normal testing with a digital capacitance meter or an analogue meter will not revealed any symptoms and you may think that the ceramic capacitor that you checked is ok. So the right way to check the ceramic capacitor leakage is to use an insulation tester. If you have the analogue insulation tester or meter, the meter panel will show a short circuit when certain voltage are applied to check the ceramic capacitor dielectrics or materials.

Testing Voltage Regulator IC

You can't test a voltage regulator IC the same way you test on other components. You have to test the voltage regulator with power "ON. You have to switch "ON" the equipment in order to accurately test voltage regulator. Identify the voltage regulator IC in circuit board first and normally it is label as IC.

Place your digital meter black probe to the equipment ground and the red probe to pin 3 of the voltage regulator IC. Power "On" the equipment and see the result. If you get 8 Volts then the IC is working fine. If you get 0 volts or 3 to 5 Volts then you have to measure the input voltage. Make sure it has more than 10 Volts input voltage. If the input voltage is lesser than 10 Volts (say 6 Volts), then suspect a fault in the power supply line or a leaky voltage regulator.

A leaky voltage regulator can pull down the input voltage. Sometimes bad components in the output line can also pull down the output voltage of regulator.

You may also desolder (remove) the output pin (pin 3) so that it will not touch the line but pin 1 and 2 is still connected. Power "ON" the equipment and check the pin 3 voltage. If there is a good input but the pin 3 output still low (say 3 Volts), most probably the voltage regulator has turned bad and need to be replaced.

Transistor Failure

Transistor can fail in a number of different ways. Transistors have forward and reverse current and voltage ratings like diodes do. Exceeding either rating can destroy a transistor. A bad transistor may short-circuit from the base to the collector or from the base to the emitter. Sometimes a transistor is damaged so badly that short circuits develop between all three of the leads. A short-circuit often allows a large current to flow, and causes the faulty transistor to heat up. The transistors also can developed open circuit between base to collector or base to emitter. The first step in identifying a bad transistor is to check for signs of overheating. A bad transistor may appear to be burnt or melted. When the equipment is switched off, you can touch the transistor to see if it feels unusually hot. The amount of heat you feel should be proportional to the size of the transistors heat sink. If the part has a large heat sink, you can expect it to be too hot but not hot enough to burn your hand or fingers. If the transistor has no heat sink, yet is very hot, you can suspect a problem.

Testing Field Effect Transistor (FET or Mosfet)

The right way of testing mosfet transistor is to use an analog multimeter. Mosfet stand for Metal oxide semiconductor field effect transistor or we just called it FET. Switch mode power supply and many other circuits use FET transistors as part of a circuit. Mosfet failure and leakage are quite high in a circuit and you need to know how to accurately test it. FET is label as "Q" in circuit board.

Measuring component's that have two leads such as the resistors, capacitors and diodes are much easier than measuring transistor and FET which have three legs. Many electronic repairers have difficulty especially checking the three leads components. First, find out the gate, drain and source pin out from semiconductor replacement book or search its datasheet from search engine. Once you have the cross reference or diagram for each pin of the mosfet, then use your analogue multimeter set to times 10K ohm range to check it. Assuming you are testing the n channel mosfet then put the black probe to the drain pin. Touch the gate pin with the red probe to discharge any internal capacitance in the mosfet. Now move the red probe to source pin while the black probe still touching the drain pin. Use your right finger and touch the gate and drain pin together and you will notice the analog multimeter pointer will move forward to center range of the meter's scale.

Use your finger to touch on the gate and drain pin. Lifting the red probe from the source pin and putting it back again to the source pin; the pointer will still remain at the middle of the meter's scale.

To discharge it you have to lift the red probe and touch just one time on the gate pin. This will eventually discharge the internal capacitance again.

If you notice that all the result that you measured kicked towards zero ohms and will not discharge, then the FET is considered shorted and need replacement. Testing the P channel FET field effect transistor is just the same way as when you check N channel FET. What you do is to switch the probe polarity when checking the P channel. Some analog multimeter have the times 100k Ohm range, this type of meter can't really test FET due to the absent of 9 Volt battery inside the multimeter. This type of meter will not have enough power to trigger the mosfet. Make sure you use a meter that has the times 10k ohm range selector.

Typical N channel mosfet part numbers are 2SK791, K1118, IRF634, IRF 740 and P channel FET transistor part number are J307, J516, IRF 9620 and etc. You can also purchase a mosfet tester online, one of the most famous brands is the SENCORE tf46 portable super cricket transistor and FET tester. You can bid one from EBay.

Wireless Issues

Wireless Issues;   **Local Access Only Issues:**

Resetting the router

To reset the router, you will simply turn the power switch on your router off and then back on after 30 seconds or so. If you use more than one router, like having a non-wireless as the main router, and a wireless router attached to the main router, you would start by just resetting the wireless router, the one at the end of your connection. Then after retesting connection, you would continue by resetting the first/main router continuing on until you have tested all routers attached. Some routers have a reset button and a power on and off switch, you can try the reset button as well, but I recommend powering on and off instead.

Troubleshooting the issue, determining if the issue is software or virus related

First and easier of the two is Software, you will start the "software ruling out" by Cleaning up the OS a little. You should start by optimizing the system configuration utility, mainly the Start Up tabs and the Services tab. Go there: Start/Run (or the search box in vista and 7), type: msconfig, press enter/ok, The system configuration utility window will pop up, there you will go to the Start Up tab, and Disable All, click apply, then navigate to the Services tab, at the bottom of that window, put a check mark in the "hide all Microsoft services" box, then choose the disable all button, click OK, and reboot the Laptop.

Check to see if the issue in question is fixed, if not continue on.

Next you will need to try booting into Safe Mode. If anything that uses network access to run was running in Normal mode, the booting into safe mode will disable it from running and allow you to make system changes. You will need administrator password to change or edit in Safe Mode, and will be limited to certain PC functions. I am not going to go into great detail about the software end, since this is a hardware repair book. To sum it up, you should be ruling out all possible software issues before having to test all the hardware components, unless the hardware is that of an obvious issue or fault.

Hard Drive Issues

Hard Drive Issues; Failing hard drives, pinpointing the issue:

Listening for issues, Clicking and grinding noise

It is common for a failing hard drive to make noise when running. This can be a few things. Typically the hard drive suffers a "head crash" and will start making a clicking sound. A head crash is when the read-write arm slams into the center platter post and slams back into the holding tray area, the click is the arm hitting the center post. When this is happening, it can scratch the platter which will cause data loss. Usually a failing hard drive will involve the read write arm, though the circuit board can fail too.

Repairing the Laptop Screen

Repairing the Laptop Screen; Front Bezel Replacing:

Removing the front bezel without breaking it

All bezels will use both snaps and screws or just snaps to secure the front bezel to the rear screen cover. The newer laptops today are just using locking plastic snaps to adhere the screen bezel or frame to the cover. If screws are used, they will have plastic or rubber screw covers over them, which are either flat or puffy stickers. Some laptops will use snaps all around the frame but still use 2 screws on the bottom of both sides, you will need to look close because the plastic screw covers are sometimes unnoticeable. You will need a plastic pry tool like a guitar pick to unsnap all the tabs on the front bezel. Start by taking the pry tool and running it along the seam between the bezel and the back panel, go up the side and back down, then run it around the corner and along the top. You are trying to poke the pry tool in between the front and back cover. Once you have a section pried open, you can continue unsnapping the front by sliding the pry tool in between then and sliding it around the top and sides. If you are having difficulty unsnapping, grab ahold with your hands and pull slightly outward towards yourself and inward towards the screen center and it should unsnap with a gently tug. You will need to free the top and 2 sides before detaching the bottom. Now to release the bottom of the bezel you can grab ahold of either corner and give a tug on it, pulling upward and inward to unsnap it. Laptops like Toshiba will release a little differently as they will need to be unsnapped in the bottom center before the corners unsnap. You would grab ahold with 2 hands on the bottom rail of the front bezel, and firmly pull towards yourself and downward at the same time, giving firm tugs on it to unsnap it... It will take a bit more force to unsnap these and they can be frustrating sometimes to unsnap, but relax and do not over pull or over tug or the plastic will break. Be careful and go slow when removing the front bezel, as it is probably the easiest part to break when removing.

Replacing a broken front bezel, choosing webcam capability for the bezel

When replacing the front bezel, it is important to find out if the series of laptop you are working on released both a webcam screen and a non-webcam screen. For some models the cover will be the same for either, but other models will use two different sized screen housings, the webcam version being slightly thicker as well as the hinges being slightly thicker. You will also need to check that the placement area of the webcam matches the replacement you are getting, some models like the HP dv9000 series will place the webcam in 3 different areas on the 17 inch screen, so if you get one with a center located webcam on the bezel and yours uses one on the left side, you will not be able to relocate the webcam to fit.

Fixing hinge lid locks that are located on the front bezel

The spring loaded hinge locks are typically located on the rear cover and poke through slots on the front bezel; some have the locks on the bezel with the spring loaded lock tab on the base or palmrest. The lock on the bezel is integrated into it, and you will need to replace the bezel to fix it. Even if you had the broken lock, I guarantee if you attempt to glue or epoxy the piece back on, it will re-break. There is just too much torque applied from the bases grabbing tab(s) that it wouldn't last.

Repairing the Laptop Screen; LCD bulb repair and replacement:

The LCD bulb plastic and aluminum housing and its importance

The CCFL bulb will be placed in a metal tray. It uses this tray to direct all the light up the plastic screen panel which is how the whole screen illuminates. The tray also helps to protect and secure the LCD bulb from breakage or heating other parts. The bulb is placed in the metal tray, then slid over the thick plastic panel and will create a sealed light environment allowing the light to only flow up the inside of the panel. The ends of the bulb will have a rubber cap over them to prevent a power short from happening, though they are removable by sliding them away or off to repair.

Repairing the Laptop Screen; LED light strip repair and replacement:

This is the new "common" light source being used, here's why...

LED lighting will give off a brighter light. It will also use less energy, taking less power to light the bulbs. LED uses a series of lights and CCFL or LCD will use one tube bulb. It is more expensive to produce but because of its popularity and need, the price will drop and it will become the "normal" making the LCD or CCFL bulb obsolete or only for the "cheap" models.

How to repair or Replace the LED light strip

LED light in a laptop uses a LED Light strip…and will have numerous tiny led bulbs that attach to a ribbon like cable… If a failure is to occur in these screens, it will typically be in the inverter/converter which is going to be located on the screens back panel, integrated onto it…Some LED Screens to have a small external inverter… if so, you will need to replace it…But for the ones that do not, you will need to replace the screen… Make note when ordering a replacement screen… the larger screens like the 16" or the 17" will use either the left or the right side for the display cable port… and if you buy the incorrect screen you might not be able to plug the display cable in, and would then need to buy an extension LED display cable which are readily available on the internet or EBAY..

Do LED screens use a power inverter? Here's your answer…

Yes and no. No there is no physical external board that the LED strip plugs into like the CCFL bulbs do. The LED Screen will have an integrated power inverter that is located on the back side of the screen. It is integrated onto the Display Panel Circuit Board. For the average 15.6 screen LED, the location will be at the opposite end of the board from where the LED light strip plugs into. If you are looking at the screen, face it so you are looking at the rear side, then flip it so the circuit board is on top, look to the left side of the circuit board and there will be a 3 inch section of components… This is the Power Inverter/Converter. On a larger 17 inch Led screen, the power controller component section is located on the right side near the area that the LED light ribbon cable plugs into. You can typically follow the traces to lead you to the power controller. You will see capacitors, diodes, resistors, a power regulator and an LED IC controller chip.

<u>**Repairing the Laptop Screen;**</u>   **Power Inverter repair and replacement**:

Determining if the inverter board is good or bad

This part will fail and the laptop will not get backlighting… And typically the transformer in the board is what fails… If you have an inverter with a similar transformer, you can solder it in place of the faulty one to revive the inverter. If that doesn't fix it, you can test the ceramic capacitors and the fuse(s) to hopefully find a fault… Otherwise it is simply easier to just replace with a new inverter… All models are available on EBAY… And will cost around $10-$20 USD. To Test the Inverter, an easy way is to attach a different LCD Bulb to it… I usually Attach the bulb from a broken screen (one that lights up, I use these because I already know it has a known working bulb in it)… And if it will light up… the inverter is good… if it will not light the bulb… the inverter needs repairing or replacing…You can as well connect a multimeter to the inverter plug end, and try to get a reading for power or no power…

But again… the easiest thing to do is to simply replace the power inverter as they are relatively cheap and readily available

Obtaining a replacement inverter

The best place to get a replacement inverter is from EBay, and will also be where you will find the cheapest prices for one. Obtain the part number from the sticker on the power inverter and enter that into the EBay search box. If no part number results show up, you can search by the Laptop model number for a replacement. Make sure the photo of the one you are purchasing matches the inverter in need of replacing exactly.

Motherboard Repair Instructions

Motherboard Repair Instructions; Tools used to test the board:

To use an anti-static wristband, or not?

I will now take a minute to discuss Anti-Static Wristband usage on Laptop Repair. I have worked on thousands upon thousands of Laptop Motherboards, and have not been shocked once. Laptop Motherboards, Printed Circuit Boards Are Self-Grounded, and do not omit static energy. In fact, I tried to use a wrist strap and have been shocked too many times to ever wear one again… You can physically touch any part of the motherboard safely without the risk of being shocked, even if the motherboard is out of the case and powered on. Unlike a Desktop Motherboard that has numerous electrolytic Capacitors and Larger Other Components that Store More Energy and can build up a Static Charge. You do not want to touch any components on the motherboard with anything Metal though, as it can short out a component by doing so (not referring to testing equipment).

Motherboard Repair Instructions; Troubleshooting the Motherboard:

MEASURING:

Voltmeter

Measuring the voltage in a circuit, we use a volt meter.

Always clamp your test pins parallel to the component you

Wish to measure. The measurement can be made anywhere

On the circuit without affecting the voltage level (Provided

You have a multimeter with good quality).

Ammeter (Amp meter)

To measure the current in a circuit, we use an Ammeter.

Always clamp your test pins in series to the components

You wish to measure (Except a clip-on ammeter).

Ohm meter

Instrument used to measure the electrical resistance of a

Conductor It is usually included in a single package with a

Voltmeter, and often an ammeter, always clamp your test

Pins in series to the components you wish to measure.

Whenever testing resistance, the circuit must be without

Voltage!

MULTIMETER

Most modern multimeters are digital and traditional analogue types are destined to become obsolete.

Here is how a typical measurement is made in typical digital multimeter nowadays:

• DC voltage: The A/D circuitry in the multimeter is designed to directly show DC voltage values typically in few volts range.

For higher voltages the input voltage is divided by a voltage divider network. For lower voltages the voltage is amplified with Amplifier.

• AC voltage: Basically same idea as the DC measurement, except that the input voltage is rectified somewhere in the process.

• DC current: Input current is run through a known low ohm resistance, which converts the input current to a small voltage drop.

This voltage is fed to the DC voltage measurement circuitry.

• AC current: This is measures in the same way as DC current, except that the voltage is fed to the AC voltage measurement

• Diode test: A low current (typically less than 1 mA) is fed to the measurement leads (output voltage limited to few volts). The

Voltage between measurement leads is measurement with DC voltage measurement electronics.

• Resistance measurement: An accurately known low current (varied depending on ohms range) is fed to the measurement leads.

The voltage (directly proportional to the resistance connected) between measurement leads is measured. Some multimeters can have some of the following functionalities in addition to the basic ones described above:

- Continuity tester: Works like the resistance measurement, if the voltage between measurements leads is lower than a specified Value (usually 50 to 300 ohms) it would make the beeper to signal

- Frequency: Input signal is converted to square wave first. The multimeter has either pulse counter (count pulses for one second gives output in Hz) or frequency to voltage converter

- Capacitance: Feed known frequency low amplitude signal through the capacitance. Measure the AC current which goes through the capacitor, other option is to measure the capacitor charge and discharge times.

- Temperature: Voltage from thermocouple sensor is amplified and processed. Then the result is fed to DC voltage measurement

Motherboard Repair Instructions;   How and What to Test, Where to start:

The Process of elimination testing

MOTHERBOARD TESTING TECHNIQUES, COMPONENT IDENTIFICATION AND LOCATIONS

Capacitor/Resistor Testing On the Motherboard

You will start testing the capacitors at the point closest to the DC Jack...then you follow in a line (imaginary line) through the motherboard... to test if power is flowing through the Motherboard...

Keep the Negative Probe Attached to a Screw Base, or touch it directly to the DC Jacks Negative Pin (the 4 side pin contacts).

While failing capacitors typically results in system instabilities, occasionally failed capacitors will lead to a failure of the voltage regulators on the motherboard. There are two common theories on why this happens.

The first (and simpler) theory is that the failing capacitors develop a very high leakage current, overloading the voltage regulators and causing them to overheat.

The second theory is that as the capacitance decreases and the ESR increases, the buck controller for the voltage regulator increases the switching frequency to compensate for the load. Since most of the MOSFET's heat output is produced during the switching transitions, the increased frequency causes them to overheat.

A capacitor rated 2200 degrees Fahrenheit may experience a drop in capacity to as little as **75 degrees Fahrenheit.** The design engineer might have assumed that it might drop up to 50% over its life, but not to 5% of its original value. The stability of the buck switching regulator is compromised by such a dramatic drop and the regulator's voltage oscillates (perhaps wildly) to voltages above the absolute maximum ratings of the ICs to which the supply is connected.

The most common failure mode of the voltage regulator is for the MOSFET to short circuit, causing the system's power supply (5 or 12 volts depending on the motherboard) to be applied directly to the CPU, Northbridge, RAM, or other components. This, in turn, causes those parts to catastrophically fail. A motherboard with symptoms of failing capacitors should be taken out of service until it is repaired in order to prevent further damage.

The Best tool for examining A Laptops motherboard is your eyes... You need to visually inspect the motherboard. Most of the time you will be able to see if a capacitor has blown or popped... you will see if a regulator chip has blown, or a mosfet has blown just by its appearance...

A LAPTOP THAT WON'T POWER ON IS LIKELY CAUSED BY A BLOWN CAPACITOR

You need to physically inspect the motherboard, using a lighted magnifying glass; you can find an exact replacement for the blown capacitor by removing one from a dead motherboard... otherwise you will need to buy some capacitors... (Not an easy find)...

Symptoms of a Blown capacitor.... When you plug in the AC Adapter, and the green power light on the adapter goes out... Resulting in No Power to the laptop...

If you find a Blown Capacitor, You need to replace it... You desolder it from the motherboard... You must be extremely careful in doing so, because if you overheat the contact pads that the capacitor connects to, you won't be able to resolder a new cap onto the motherboard...

Add a Tiny amount of Flux paste to each end of the Cap, then use a thin desoldering braid (solder wick) and touch the end of the Cap with it, take your soldering gun and touch it to the desoldering braid - then touching the capacitor end to remove the thin layer of solder covering it... you don't need to remove all the solder.... Do this once again to the opposite end....

Now you use a Micro-Sized Flat Head Screwdriver and gently touch the side of the capacitor (you will be pushing on the Cap to remove it), Touch your soldering guns tip to the end of the Capacitor, and at the same time, gently apply pressure with the screwdriver to the side of the Cap to push it sideways off its Pad. Heat the End to melting point ... then quickly switch to the opposite end and heat... the capacitor will "Pop" Off and Roll off its Pad. Now you can solder a New One On...

NOTE: I use a Black Permanent Marker When Removing a Capacitor... Color the TOP of the Capacitor All Black... this way, when you remove the capacitor - you will know which side is the top...

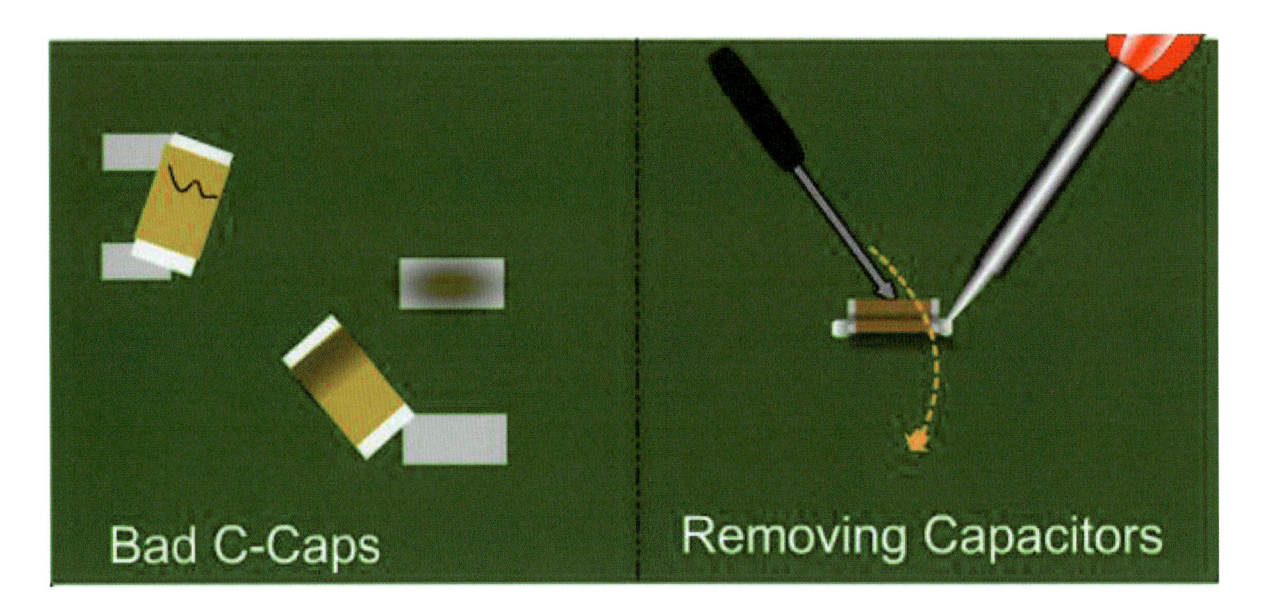

Motherboard Testing Procedures

Compared to aluminum electrolytics, tantalum capacitors have very stable capacitance, little DC leakage, and very low impedance at high frequencies. However, unlike aluminum electrolytics, they are intolerant of positive or negative voltage spikes and are destroyed (often exploding violently) if connected in the circuit backwards or exposed to spikes above their voltage rating.

An ESR meter is an electronic measuring instrument which measures the equivalent series resistance of capacitors without disconnecting them from circuit.

An example of testing Mosfets: I use an In Circuit ESR Meter (Capacitor Wizard), Placing One Probe on The Top End Pin, then moving the bottom probe from pin 1 thru to 4, Making sure to hear the ESR Meter BEEP and Read "Good"...

OLPC XO-1.5 B1 Prototype

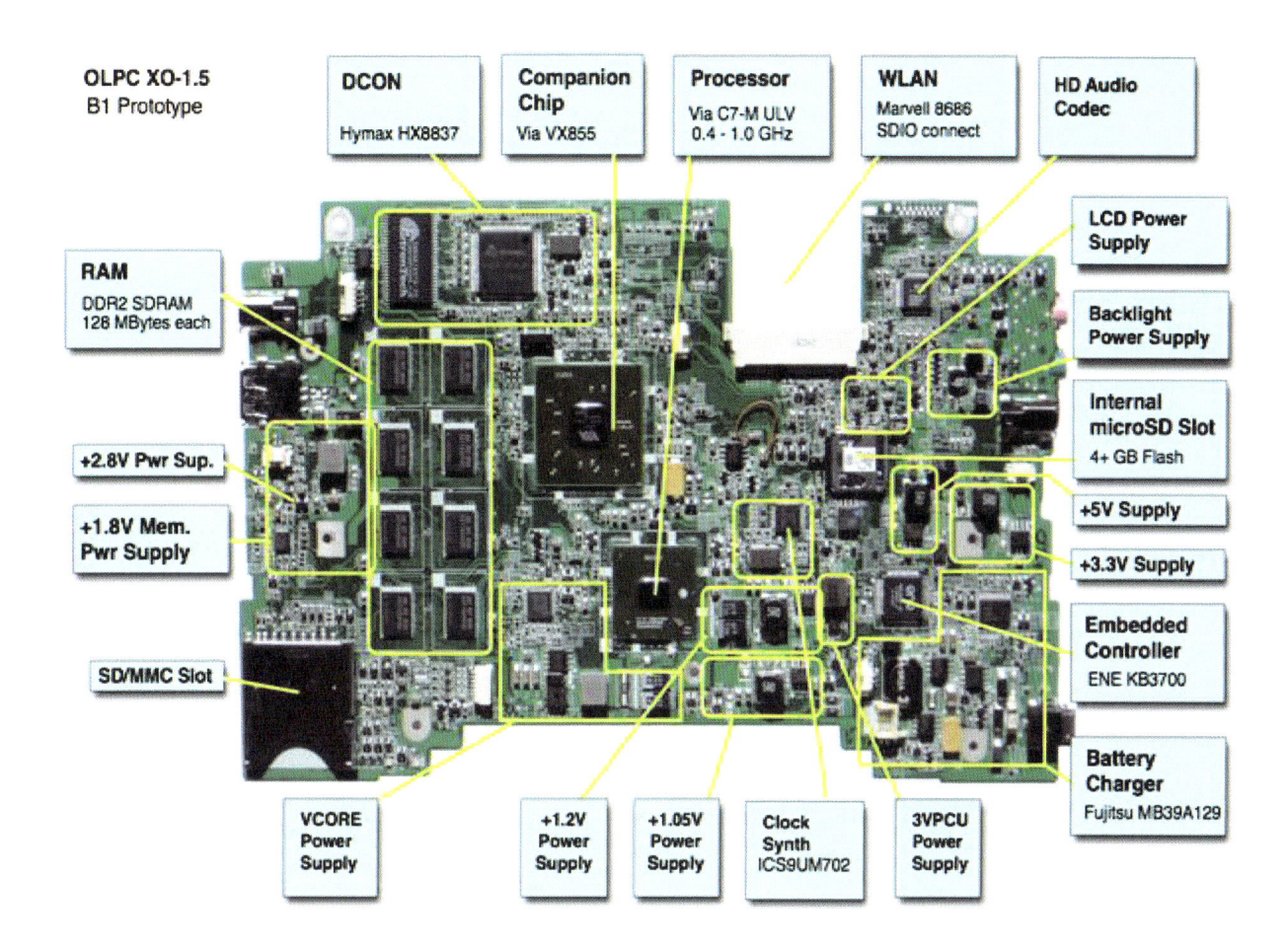

- DCON — Hymax HX8837
- Companion Chip — Via VX855
- Processor — Via C7-M ULV 0.4 - 1.0 GHz
- WLAN — Marvell 8686 SDIO connect
- HD Audio Codec
- LCD Power Supply
- Backlight Power Supply
- Internal microSD Slot — 4+ GB Flash
- +5V Supply
- +3.3V Supply
- Embedded Controller — ENE KB3700
- Battery Charger — Fujitsu MB39A129
- 3VPCU Power Supply
- Clock Synth — ICS9UM702
- +1.05V Power Supply
- +1.2V Power Supply
- VCORE Power Supply
- SD/MMC Slot
- +1.8V Mem. Pwr Supply
- +2.8V Pwr Sup.
- RAM — DDR2 SDRAM 128 MBytes each

Testing the Motherboard

No Power to Laptop, what to test for:

Note: // Testing All Motherboards Is a Process of Elimination...Ruling out one thing... going to the next in line possibility...

First thing to check is the AC Adapter (the charger)...Use a multimeter for this, put the black negative prod on the outside of the plug tip, and put the red positive prod on the inside of the plug tip...

Next check the DC Jack

There are 2 general types of DC Jacks... Onboard.... and Off-board/Extended

The onboard dc jacks, the ones that are directly soldered to the motherboard are typically the ones that fail. The Off board or the ones that use a wire connection and rest in a slot in the case... Are 100 times more stable... because they are able to move slightly if needed when over-torque is applied....

You need to visually inspect the pins on the DC Jack from both sides of the motherboard... If the Jack is faulty, you can usually see the melted solder/missing solder/burn-out spot/short...If the Jack and Pin

Connections Look Good then it's time to test with multimeter... You need to test the pin area, and surrounding ceramic capacitors/Fuses.

DC Jack Is Good, What Next?

Next you need to make absolutely sure all Hardware is functioning properly...

Test The Hard Drive, Test Your RAM, and Test Your CPU (though this is typically not the issue)

Motherboard Repair Instructions;   The Components on the motherboard:

Resistors

Resistors and types of resistors: What is a resistance?

The property of a substance, which opposes the flow of an electric current through it, is called a resistance. It's is measured in ohms and is represented by letter 'R'

Each resistor has two main characteristics.

1) Its resistance value in ohms and 2) its power dissipating capacity in watts

Resistors are employed for many purposes such as electric heaters, telephone equipment's, electric and electronic circuit elements and in current limiting devices. As resistors are used in wide applications there values like power rating, R value, tolerance etc. vary. Resistors of resistance value ranging from .1ohms to many mega ohms are manufactured. Acceptable tolerance levels range from +/- 20% to as low as +/-.001%. The power rating may be as low as 1/10 watts and can be in several hundred watts. These all vary in range and type of application a particular resistor is used.

Classification of Resistors:

From operating conditions point of view, resistors can be classified into two.

1) Fixed resistors

2) Adjustable/ variable resistors

1) Fixed resistors are further classified into:

a) Carbon composition type resistors b) Metalized type resistors c) Wire wound type resistors

a) Carbon composition type resistors:

This is the most common type of low wattage resistor. The resistive material is of carbon-clay composition and the leads are made of tinned copper. These resistors are cheap and reliable and stability is high.

b) Wire wound resistors:

These resistors are a length of wire wound an insulating cylindrical core. Usually wires of material such as constantan (60% copper and 40% nickel) and manganin which have high resistivities and low temperature coefficients are employed. The completed wire wound resistor is coated with an insulating material such as baked enamel.

c) Metalized resistors

It is constructed using film deposition techniques of depositing a thick film of resistive material onto an insulating substrate. Only approximate values of resistance can be had by this method.

2) Variable resistors

For circuits requiring a resistance that can be adjusted while it remains connected in the circuit (for ex: volume control on radio), variable resistors are required. They usually have 3 lead two fixed and one movable.

LAPTOP COMPONENTS

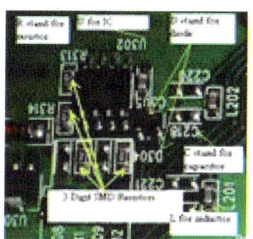

Audio Controller Chip   **Bridge Rectifiers**   **Component Guide**   **Crystal Oscillators**

Digital Audio I-face Receivers   **Flash Memory IC**   **Flash Memory**

Host Controller IC   **IC OP Amp Dual**   **IC Voltage**

COMPONENT IDENTIFICATION CONTINUED...

DDPAK	DPAK	DIP	SQP	SW	T7-TO220
FDIP	PDIP	PENTAWATT	TO220	TO2205	TO220ISO
PLCC	QDIP	QFP	TO252	TO263	TO268
SIP	SO	SO8	TO3	TO52	TO99
SOT223	SOT23	SQL	TSOP	ZIP	

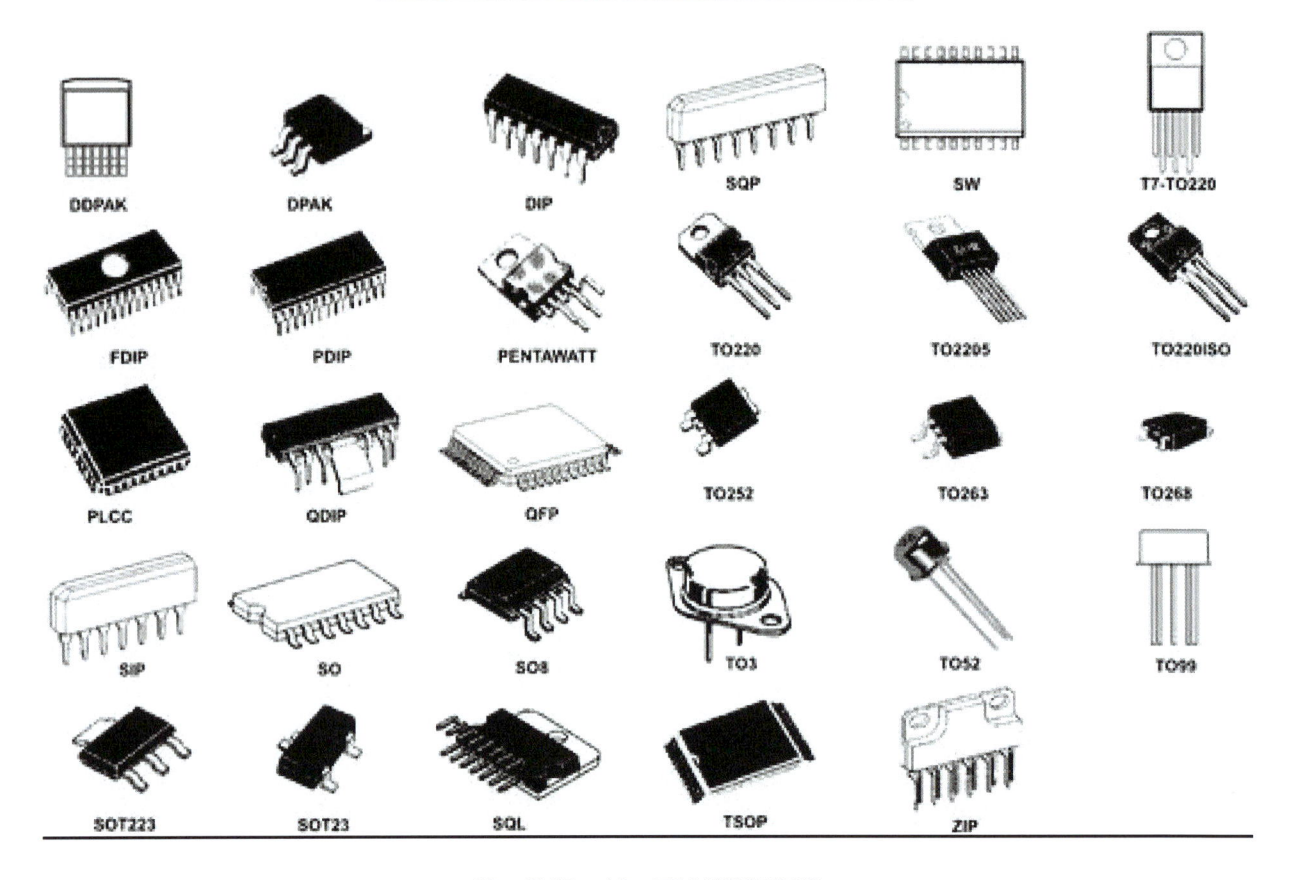

IC – SMD – IC – TRANSISTORS

COMPONENT IDENTIFICATION CONTINUED...

8-Lead MSOP and SOIC
(RM-8 and R-8 Suffixes)

NULL — 1   8 — NC
−IN — AD8610 — V+
+IN —   — OUT
V− — 4   5 — NULL

NC = NO CONNECT

Jfet OP AMP Schematics　　　**Jfet OP Amp**

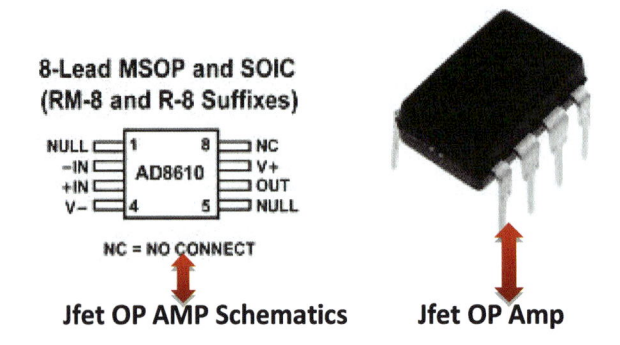

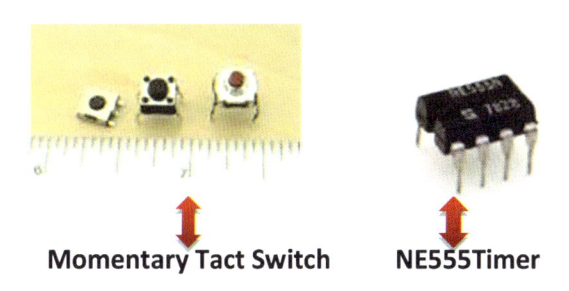

Momentary Tact Switch   **NE555Timer**

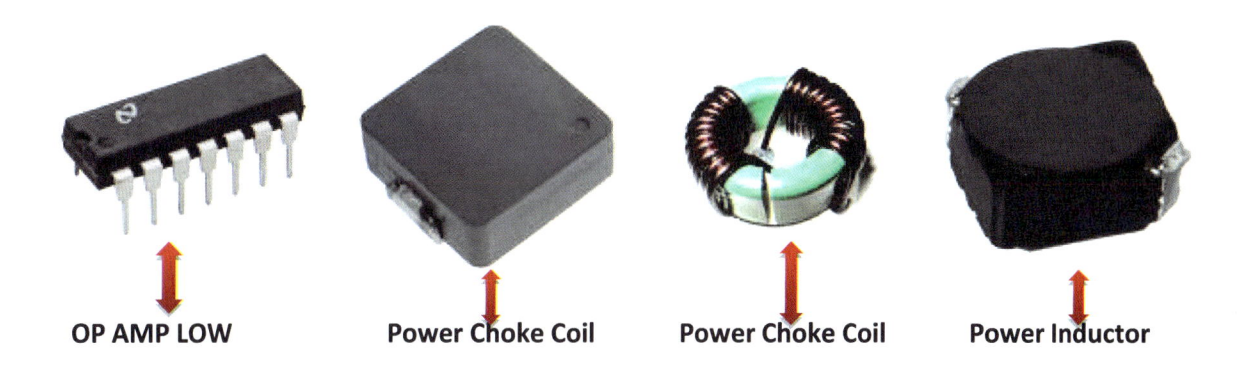

OP AMP LOW   **Power Choke Coil**   **Power Choke Coil**   **Power Inductor**

COMPONENT IDENTIFICATION CONTINUED…

Power Inductor 1 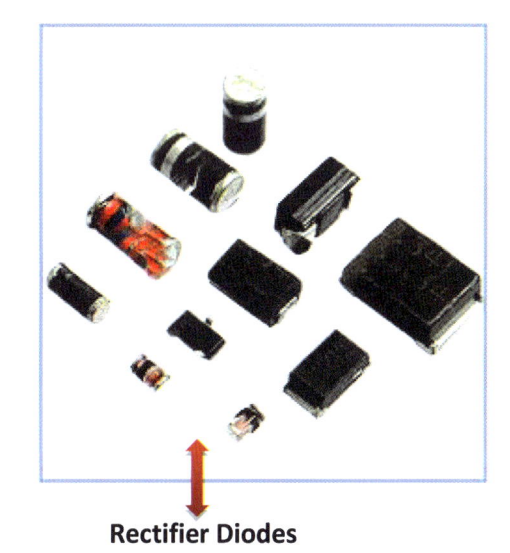   **Rectifier Diodes**

Resettable Fuse

Resettable Fuses

Resistor Array

Resistor

SATA Controller IC

Shielded Power Inductor

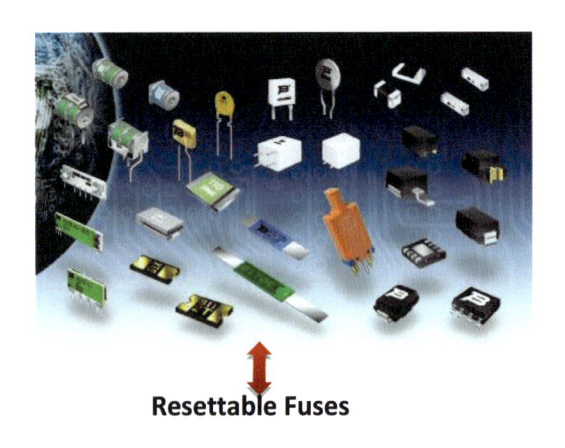

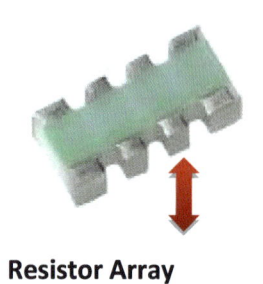

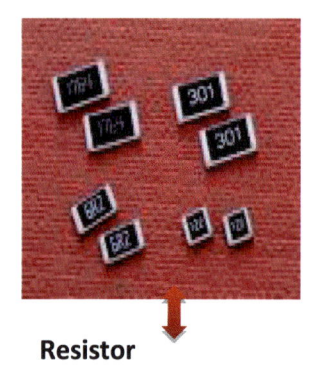

Single Coil Relay

SMD Electrolytic Capacitor

LAPTOP COMPONENTS CONTINUED...

SMD Power Inductor Types

COMPONENT IDENTIFICATION CONTINUED...

SOIC   Switching Diode   Switching Diode 1

Tantalum Capacitors  **Triple 3 Input NAND CMOS**

TXCO Voltage Controller  **USB Controller Chip** 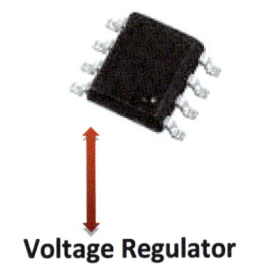 **Voltage Regulator**

<u>**Motherboard Repair Instructions;**</u>   **PCB (printed circuit board) Repair Methods:**

Repairing damaged traces on the motherboard

You will First Clean and Scrape the area to Prep for the New Trace. Use alcohol pad to wipe the board after gently scraping the area with your Razor blade knife. You want to carefully scrape the epoxy off of the trace on both sides of the missing area to be able to reconnect both sides using your Conductive Silver Trace Pen. Draw a thin line using the Silver Trace Pen (bought off Ebay), then go over the line if needed to ensure a proper connection. Let dry, if able to, you can go over the new trace repair with a thin line of solder. You can now use an Overcoating pen to insulate your repair. Overcoating will paint a layer similar to the green coating currently on the motherboard and can be bought in colors to match the motherboards color.

Repairing damaged pin contacts, eye rings, C-Ring repair techniques

Damage to the DC Jack's Pin Contact Pads and C-Ring

These Center Copper Rings are located inside the holes of the dc jack pin ports and ensure proper contact from the upper side of the motherboard to the lower side, and layers within.

If they Come Out During the DC Jack Removal, Or if They Already Had ripped out due to wear and tear (usually happens to the Center Positive Pin) then You Can attempt to use the one from the Jack that it is stuck to or if you have thin copper sheet, you can cut and shape new ones... But if that isn't an option for you, you can scrape around the edge of the pin hole until the copper layer is showing, tin that area and hope it gives a strong enough connection.

You can purchase Copper Tape that comes with an adhesive backing, it is sold in rolls, if you can find around 10 feet worth, you will have plenty to work with. It can be used to seal the fan and heatsink too.

To shape the copper ring needed to replace the missing one on the motherboard, you would cut a piece off the roll. You will use a Pin (or Sewing needle) to wrap the copper foil around to make the tube shape needed for the dc jack port repair. You want just enough copper to make a perfect circle, try not to overlap the copper. And you will want it 1.5mm long. Once made, keep it affixed to the pin head to be able to easily insert it on the motherboard for the repair.

Place the copper tube that you just made in the hole/slot and remove the pin... Use that same pin to widen the ends/edges on both sides of the motherboard... do this by using just the tip of the pin or needle, and hold it at an angle. You are basically trying to round off the edge of the copper ring so that it bends over the lip of the motherboard slightly and tight.

Then you will flux the area of the contact pad, and tin it with soldering tin, then apply a thin layer of solder to the contact pad.

Re-insulating the motherboard (the green or blue color Overcoat sealant)

To repair the motherboard overcoat, you can purchase a pen that will allow you to paint the area in need of repair. It is sold on EBay and is available in either green or blue. It is called "Overcoat Pen" by Techspray Corporation, part number: 2509-GN. To start, you will shake the pen to mix the overcoat, then, take a scrap piece of paper and practice flowing the paint; it is made to paint a very thin line if needed, so ensure that you have the pen flowing good before starting the repair. Now you will apply the overcoat to the specific area in need of repair only, do not cover any component trace. To repair a scratch, you would simply draw over the crack, wait 2 minutes and do a second coat, then a third. The deeper the damaged area, the more layers you will add to result in a level smooth surface.

Replacing a damaged component

Upon finding a damaged or faulty component, you must remove that component and replace it with an exact component part. Let's take for example that you discover a ceramic capacitor (brownish-tan in color) has blown, you now will need to replace that capacitor, but how? You don't have another one to put in its place. Well, you will have 2 choices here, you will either need to remove the component needed from a different motherboard, or you will have to purchase that component on the internet, and I say over the internet because you will never find a component replacement part locally, they are not sold in stores. If you are a repair technician, it would be a good idea to save every one of the faulty motherboards you come in contact with. You will find that they come in use when a component is needed to be pulled from it to repair an existing issue.

You can sometimes find PCB components in the internet, you can get the numbers off of the component and use Google search to locate any available. Chances are that whoever is selling the component on the web will require that you buy that component in "bulk", meaning you will need to buy a large quantity just to get the one you need.

If you happen to have "non-working" motherboards you can search the motherboards for an exact replacement Ceramic Capacitor. It has to be the same size (length, width, height), and the same tone or color. When replacing the capacitor, try to keep the capacitor that you have removed in the same position that it came off the board as. Then assuming you have already removed the faulty capacitor, you can replace the bad with the good cap. To remove the capacitor, you will apply flux paste to both ends of the capacitor, then tin the soldering gun tip and touch the tip to one side of the faulty capacitor, take it to melting point; you will visually see the change from solid to liquid, then quickly remove the tip and go to the opposite side and repeat. Now take your micro sized flat head screwdriver and gently pry from the side of the capacitor while heating the cap ends alternating from one end to the other, take your time and eventually you will have both ends soft enough that when you are prying on the capacitors side wall, it will free itself from the solder contact pads and will remove from the board. When replacing the component, you will flux the empty contact pads and flux the new caps ends lightly. Place the capacitor onto the contact pads and us ether flat head micro screwdriver to hold it in place. It is important to hold the component in place otherwise when the solder gun tip touches it, it will adhere to the tip and you will have to start all over.

Board-Flex repair and prevention

Something you might encounter is Motherboard Flex or Warp, This is when the motherboard is physically damaged due to either heat exposure warping the pcb.... or by flexing of the motherboard, due to the laptops poor design and it will actually move inside the case to the point where the traces running through the PCB will crack/break... causing Motherboard Failure. A lot of times, poor hinge design will cause this...some laptop designs can't take the torque that it takes to open and firmly hold the screens, and over extended usage will flex the motherboard in a wiggling fashion...It can be near impossible to find the exact point of fault in a board flex issue because it will usually affect the internal layers of the motherboard, or it will damage the underside of the IC chip or its connection, which will be virtually undetectable with current testing tools. If you had access to an X-ray machine, you would be able to easily locate flex faults. To prevent board flex, you can ensure all the screws are tight. You will not be able to "mod" in any sort of brace, you can however, try using pressure point repairing, where you can use a rubber shoe, like the ones on the bottom side of the laptop, to press down on that area of the board which should prevent future flexing when the palmrest or base is reinstalled and the rubber brace is sandwiched between the board and the upper or lower base. If doing this, you do not want to use an oversized rubber piece; you want it to be basically the same height as the gap in between the board it is adhering to and the upper or lower base.

Hard Drive Repairing

Hard Drive Repairing;   Disassembling the Hard Drive:

Removing the screws to replace the circuit board card

The circuit board on the bottom of every hard drive will have a series of screws securing it to the housing. Typically the screw type will be a star tip, and you will use a star tipped screwdriver to remove the viewable screws. There are no hidden screws on the circuit board side, so once you have removed all the screws you can pull the board away from the housing. Pull straight outward away from the case because the connection black plastic port that connects the board to the hard drive, will need to slide out of the port. Once the screws are removed, it is easiest if you use a plastic pry tool to pull the board away from the case, then grab ahold and pull away.

Removing the screws to disassemble the cover to gain access to the inner components

When removing the metal plate cover, you will most likely encounter star tipped screws used to secure the cap. There will also usually be one screw that resides under the white label sticker. This screw can be found by running your finger around the sticker to feel the indented circular area; the screw is in the center of the circular area. Instead of peeling the sticker off, just poke the screwdriver tip through the sticker to unscrew the screw. The screw is usually located to the bottom left, its purpose is to secure the platters center post to the upper half (cover). All the other screws are visible and are around the outer edge of the cover, remove all. Grab any area of the metal cover and pull it away from the hard drive.

Hard Drive Repairing;   What to look for inside the hard drive:

The parts that make up a hard drive, the location and their uses

The Disc Platters: The platters are the physical discs inside that store the magnetized data. The platter surfaces are coated with a thin film that stabilizes the magnetically reactive particles that are spread across the disk. Platters are divided into tracks (concentric circles) and sectors (track segments). Platters are made out what is called a substrate, which is an aluminum alloy material.

The Read/Write Arm(s): This actuator arm has a triangular shaped magnet/ voice coil at the opposite end of the heads, which is also connected to a spring mechanism, the spring will ensure the head arm actuator bounces back to the skid, and the magnet will react to the current flow from the power source to move the arm magnetically.

The Spindle Motor: This is what the platters connect to and is what allows the platters to spin evenly. It is a disc shaped motor and is built in levels, the bottom base , the first level, being the largest "circle" that allows the platters an even lip to rest on, then the spacer (if needed) then the cap.

The Read/Write Heads: These are connected to small metal suspension arms that will float over the platter surface though not touching the surface.

Debris Catcher Pad: The base of the inside will have a wall shaped around the spinning platter, this keeps the platter area isolated, and the walls will direct any debris towards the catcher pad. This pad will catch particles smaller than the eye can view, it will also prevent a static buildup around the spinning platters.

The Arm Skids or Trays: These are made of plastic and are the area where the read/write arm heads will rest when in idle or off. The screw can be loosened slightly to realign the track to allow for a smooth landing of the arm if by chance it should misalign itself from vibration. It can have multiple levels for the multiple read/write arm layers.

Hard Drive Repairing;   **Repairing Hard Drive Failure Issues**:

Transfer of the disc/data platters

To retrieve data from a hard drive that has failed, you can attempt to pull the platters and swap them into a new assembly. You will need to get a duplicate hard drive, the same size and the same manufacturer. The internals must be exactly the same. This needs to be the same because if slightly different, the platters will not fit. The platter thickness will also vary depending on the size of the hard drive and also by the manufacturer's specifications. Take for instance you have a 320GB hard drive that has 2 platters in it. You will need to swap both of these platters over, and if you attempt to install them in a 120GB hard drive that only uses one platter, it will not fit.

Speaker and Audio Issues

Speaker and Audio Issues;   **No sound from speakers or from headphone jack**:

The first thing to do is to reinstall the most current driver software update

For your Laptops driver update, there is no need to uninstall any current drivers. You will need to go to the website of your laptops manufacturer to get the current audio or multimedia driver. Once at the main page (ex: www.hp.com or www.dell.com, or www.toshiba.com) you will look for the drivers and downloads section or link.   You will be directed to enter the laptops model number or series number to direct you to specific driver sets, once there. You will see all the drivers for your laptop, like, audio, video, network and so on. Pick the current driver available in the audio section for your driver and install it. If it is not the correct driver, it will not install and you will get an error pop up message, to which you will need to search there for a different audio driver, or choose an earlier version of windows from the choice list. If asked to restart your Laptop when the driver install completes, go ahead and do so. Go into the control panel then into the device manager to check for proper installation of the driver.

Visual inspection of the motherboard, speaker and port connections

If you have attempted a driver update and still have no sound, you will need to visually inspect the components. Look at the audio out ports, the headphone and microphone jacks, look for blackened areas, look for broken parts. You can proceed to disassembling the laptop to reveal the motherboard and the speakers. Look for blown woofer cones, look for cracked pinched or broken speaker or audio wires. Examine the motherboard, looking for blown components or for possible water damage. Slightly wiggle the speaker wires right where they plug into the motherboard, do this while attempting to play an audio file on the laptop if able to. If able to connect a replacement speaker set into the motherboard, do so to see if that fixes the issue. If still having issues after trying the previous testing and repair techniques, you most likely have an irreversible issue on the motherboard and will need to change the board to fix the issue.

Speaker and Audio Issues;   Replacing the Speakers:

Unplugging the speakers, cleaning the speakers

To clean the speakers, once again, you are to use the toothbrush, preferably a soft bristled one… and gently go over the speakers using a circular motion.

Determining speaker failure issues

AUDIO PORT REPAIR, LOSS OF AUDIO FROM INTERNAL SPEAKERS AND FROM AUDIO JACK PORT(s)

No Sound Coming From the Laptop's Speakers

Audio Loss can on rare occasion be caused by 3rd party software or even virus/Trojans, so you should rule out these things prior to proceeding.

The first thing you need to do here is to assume that it is a Software / Driver issue. Try going to the laptops manufacturers website and downloading ALL the Listed drivers for your current Operating System. Reboot the computer and see if anything has changed. Go into your device manager (in the Control Panel) and look to see if there are any errors or missing drivers or driver conflicts.

If that did not work, Try Uninstalling your Audio driver from the device manager, then reboot and let windows search and load the most compatible driver found.

If still No Audio, the motherboard will need to be examined, you need to physically look at the speakers, the speaker wires and the plugs, make sure the wires are not pinched or cut. If still no audio, you most likely have A Controller Chip Issue and nothing will correct the audio… you will need to replace the motherboard.

Another option you have now is a USB add on sound/audio card which is about the size of a mini thumb drive or flash drive. You plug it into an empty USB slot and from there; you can plug in either speakers, or headphones through the 2 ports on the plug.

How to replace blown speakers

You will need to get exact replacement speakers if they are not working or blown. These can be bought off EBay and will come in a set of both left and right unless the speakers are housed in a single unit. Some laptops have built in sub woofers, and these as well can be replaced easily. The most difficult will be disassembling the laptop to get to the speakers for removal. When ordering, or finding replacement speakers, you will search by the laptop model number, not by the speaker part number. If no replacements are available, you can attempt to repair the speaker if possible, it will all depend on the issue it is having as to whether it has a chance of a successful repair. For a blown speaker cone, you can try rubber cement to repair, for bad wire connection, you can resolder a new wire set, but typically when the speakers fail, they will need to be replaced, not repaired.

Hard Drive Repairing;   Determining failure of the controller chip on the motherboard:

Process of elimination testing conclusion

DIAGNOSING AND REPAIRING A FAILING HARD DRIVE, AND RETRIEVING DATA

What Does a Clicking or Buzzing Noise Mean?

Though some older hard drives will tend to run "noisy", it will usually indicate that the drive has suffered from a "Head Crash". This happens when the Read/Write Arm has slammed into the center disc rail and then bounced back to the holding tray and most likely has bent/ misaligned the arm reader tips to the point where they cannot read/write...

How to Repair:

Only way to repair this issue is to either replace the read/write arm assembly, or to pull the Platters out and swap them into an exact hard drive make/model with known "good" arm assembly. You MUST use an exact replacement Drive if swapping the Components...

A Failing Hard Drive Still Has a Chance That DATA Can Be Retrieved before It Is Completely "dead"

Remove the hard drive from the laptop, Connect it by using a USB to sata drive adapter (which can be bought off of EBay for a couple of dollars, or you can also use one from a mini external hard drive enclosure) Then Open My Computer in the Laptop or Computer that you are connecting the Drive To, and Wait for the Hard Drive Icon To Appear.

Avoid using those Online Data Retrieval Companies

The amount of money those companies charge for attempting to Get Your Data from Damaged Platters is Outrageous! And in most cases that I've seen, the Company ends up not being able to get the data ... They Charge Thousands of Dollars for The Service, and in My Opinion, and It Is NOT worth it, call it a LOSS and Start a New...

Removable Media

Removable Media;   SD Cards, SSD, USB Devices, Flash Drives, Thumb Drives, External Hard Drives:

Description of the most common types of removable media

Flash drives are the most convenient of the commonly used devices, as they are the most portable due to their size. They are increasing in size allowing enough space even for full system back-ups. The downfall of these devices is the chance for failure and total data loss. Once these devices fail, it is virtually impossible to revive or to retrieve any data.

The external hard drive would be the most popular of the bunch, it can save your back-ups and due to the sizes available, can store whatever you desire with room to spare. There is less chance of failure with these devices though the possibility does exist that failure will occur. You can get external drives currently in the 2.5 or the 3.5 size.

SSD Cards are more of a permanent media, though removable if needed easily. They are the newest type of data storage and have been recently added to the Laptop/Notebook/Netbook families. They do not create heat and are the side of a Wi-Fi card. This allows for fan-less netbook designs to be possible, and its size allows for other needed parts and components to be added instead of left out, giving the netbooks almost the same capabilities as the Laptop.

Laptop Add On Components

Laptop Add On Components; Cooling Pads, Plug In USB Devices, Accessories:

Some common add on components

SD memory cards, mini SD, thumb drives/flash drives, Wi-Fi PC cards, USB fans, USB gadgets, Hubs, Docking Stations, Phone docks, modems, USB sound cards, access points, and the list is endless.

Liquid Spills to the Laptop

Liquid Spills to the Laptop; Steps to take to prevent future damage:

How To Repair a Laptop/Notebook That Has Had Liquid Spilled On It

This is a Tough Repair to Handle... But I have had great success in repairing motherboards that receive Liquid damage... And I'm here to share my knowledge with you...

Many types of liquid can/will spill onto Laptops, the most common being, water, beer, milk, wine, and juice.

Each of these liquids cause damage, though each will cause damage in different ways.

THE FIRST THING TO DO WHEN LIQUID HAS SPILLED ONTO/INTO LAPTOP

Unplug the Laptop, and remove the Battery. You want to disconnect all power sources from the laptop.

Leaving the battery in will allow the motherboard to continue to short out, causing further damage and possible irreversible damage.

Flip the Laptop To The Opposite Side That The Spill Entered... So If the spill occurred on the keyboard area... you would open the laptop and flip it face down, the keyboard side down... to allow remaining liquid to drain out the same way it came in...

Any Laptop that has suffered from liquid spill should be completely disassembled and inspected.

Each Specific Liquid will appear differently on the Motherboard and depending how long it has been there and if power was still on when the spill occurred, it will also show signs of corrosion.

This is what you will be looking for (corrosion)... with water, it will appear as a whitish color and kind of Powdery...

I use a product called CRC Electrical Grade 2-26 precision Lubricant Spray to start My Motherboard Corrosion Cleaning Process.

I use a Soft - Bristled Toothbrush to initially clean the motherboard... applying a light amount of the spray to the bristles... The Toothbrush won't ruin the motherboard, nor will it rip off any capacitors or other components... And It Will Safely Remove the Corrosion and Help to prevent it from returning...

You want to inspect both sides of the motherboard, Start at the DC Jack Area, Look at the solder pins of the jack to see if any white powdery substance exists, or possibly shorted pin connections... then you will start by looking at all the Capacitors, you might need a magnifying glass to get a close view.. Look in the RAM (DIMM) Ports, looking at the gold pins to see if any have a tarnished look or again a powdery substance on them... clean the pins with the toothbrush...

Use the CRC 2-26 spray on the toothbrush bristles, then dab the toothbrush onto a piece of paper towel to remove some of the spray (you don't want the toothbrush to be "wet".. it should have a very tiny amount of the spray on it... then back and forth motion over the capacitors/resistors/mosfets etc.. that have visible corrosion..

Then go over the area you scrubbed with the toothbrush using a piece of paper towel... dab the motherboard gently to pull up any remaining spray on the motherboard...you don't need to completely dry the board, and it is ok if the motherboard still has a slight wet appearance after scrubbing and dabbing it dry... The spray is non-conductive and will dissipate eventually...

You need to also check the port that your video display cable plugs into on the motherboard... Look into it for any corroded pins, clean with toothbrush... Look at the display cable plug end too, and clean if necessary... If you know where the liquid initially spilled, then you can usually direct your motherboard cleaning to that specific area... But if you don't know, and all liquid has already dried, then I suggest you go over the whole motherboard with the toothbrush and spray. They Do Sell Circuit Board Cleaner at Electronic Stores, But I've had such good success with the fore-mentioned spray that it is all I use...

If you are a Serious Repair Tech, I recommend you purchase something called: "Capacitor Wizard"

This is a Laptop Technicians Must Have Tool!! It will test your "in circuit" Capacitors... And Will give accurate immediate results...Will tell you the bad ones and will tell you the good ones... No more taking hours upon hours using a multimeter, No more finding a Stable Negative Post and No More Misdiagnosed capacitors!! Will test other components on the motherboard as well... When using this meter, I can fully test a Motherboard in a matter of a couple minutes... With my Digital Multimeter, It Took Me hours, Sometimes Days, And Still I Was Left Wondering on some using the multimeter...But not with the Capacitor Wizard... as it measures differently than a Multimeter... It measures ESR... (Equivalent Series Resistance) And the Meter Probes Are Non-Polar...

Removing the Battery, the AC Adapter and why

The very first thing you must do when a liquid spill occurs, or when you first notice that one has, is to remove all power sources to the laptop. Unplug it first, then pull the battery out and set aside until the internal components can be examined and potential damage ruled out.

Keyboard Covers

You can find keyboard covers all over the internet and they are relatively cheap. Some will be an exact fit, and some will cover the keyboard and overlap onto the palmrest securing itself to the plastic using double sided tape.

These are good to prevent potential liquid spills from harming components, and good for keeping food particles out of the keyboard. They however, can be annoying to use and some people just don't like the feeling of them, so it is the users choice whether to use or not to use.

Liquid Spills to the Laptop; Cleaning the Remaining Liquid:

Materials and cleaning solutions used to remove the liquid spill residue

CRC Electrical Grade 2-26 precision Lubricant Spray

WD-40 (Part Cleaner and lubricant)

Liquid No Residue Flux (will remove existing corrosion on solder)

Denatured Alcohol (will clean the planer board or PCB)

Electronic Circuit Board Cleaner (available at electronics stores like Radio-Shack (*USA*) or similar)

Knowing what spilled by its appearance

This is something that will be better explained by experience, the more often you see liquid spills, the better you will become at determining exactly what the liquid is by its appearance. Clear liquids like water or clear juices will leave a whitish and bluish colored film on the motherboard and will remain in puddles even when evaporated. If all the liquid has dissipated, it will appear to be an outline of the liquid pool that once sat there, and will look and feel powdery. The medium color liquids like coffee and milk will tend to leave a sticky milky residue, and will sometimes appear this way for months if left unattended. The darker liquids like red juice, black coffee, red wine and similar will leave a mix between the clear and the medium. They will sometimes look like dried up black tar, or will dry in a thin pool and appear as evaporated black or brown stained areas with a wavy appearance. The darker liquids like the medium liquids will take longer to dissipate and will "coat" components with a film that attracts the corrosion process and will speed up the deterioration process to that area or part.

Cleaning the keyboard

This can be a hit or miss repair, the task involves taking the entire keyboard apart key by key, hinge by hinge, then peeling off the protective films to access the key contact pad. If you have gotten this far and still have not broken any pieces, you can use a slightly damp cloth (not water, use denatured alcohol) and when I say slightly damp, I mean enough to pull any residue of liquid but dry enough not to leave any liquid after wiping. When liquid damage occurs to the keyboard area, I will always just replace the keyboard, ordering a replacement off of EBay, they average under $20.00*USD*. If by chance the clean-up did not resolve any keyboard failure issues, you will need to replace the keyboard.

Liquid Spills to the Laptop;   What happens if left unattended:

Component corrosion sets in

Components on the motherboard will succumb to liquid damage and it may take a bit of time before the chemical reaction becomes visible. It will happen a lot quicker if electricity is still flowing through the motherboard, though will still happen if all power sources are removed. The corrosion will typically attack the solder joints or connections that attach the component to the motherboard. Clear liquids will resemble leaky battery acid, kind of a powdery whiteish-blueish color, while dark liquids like red wine or cola, coffee and similar will also show a powdery substance, it will be darker in color and can sometimes look black in appearance. The longer it is left unattended with a power source attached, the more chance the motherboard will have at sustaining permanent damage, such as blown fuses, blown regulators, blown capacitors and so on. You will need to closely inspect the motherboard, looking everywhere to locate any traces of liquid. Note here that you are not necessarily looking for liquid in its liquid state… you are also looking for the remnants of dissipated liquid which will leave distinctive markings when dried up. Water or clear liquids will leave a pool of white or the outline of white and will be somewhat powdery in appearance. Dark liquids will remain more visible when dissipated, and will appear as a brown sticky substance.

The damage it causes and prolonged damage common to a liquid spill

If left unattended and not thoroughly removed, it will start eating away at the solder connections of the components, and then will eat away at the component itself. It can both stop or block the power to a series of components, or it can physically blow the component shorting it out by connecting both ends together and arcing it out. It will even start eating away at the PCB if given enough time and if the right components are damaged. Liquid can travel under IC chips on the motherboard and create heat puddles that can blow out the chip, and it can also travel under BGA chipsets and cause damage and failure to the chips connection. The corrosion will tend to be heaviest where active power is flowing through the board, the chemical change of the liquid substrate will occur faster given a constant voltage current.

Liquid Spills to the Laptop;   Repairing any damage caused by the spill:

Proper way to remove the corrosion that resides on the components after a spill

CRC Electrical Grade 2-26 precision Lubricant Spray is the best at cleaning the remnants of corrosion, it not only removes the existing corrosion, it also helps to prevent it from returning. Apply a small amount onto a soft bristled toothbrush and apply gently to the areas needed using a small circular motion. Liquid flux will also quickly loosen and remove corrosion occurring on components.

Testing and replacing damaged components

With a liquid damaged component, you will most likely be able to visually see the damage and can instantly determine if it is in need of being replaced as opposed to being cleaned. You will remove the component and proceed to thoroughly clean the area after removal. You will then re-inspect the cleaned area for further unnoticed damage that might have occurred. If you can then determine that the contact pads or lands are in good shape, you can proceed to replace that faulty component with an exact replacement part. I cannot stress enough that the replacement component must be an exact part replacement.

Baking the motherboard to dissipate the residual liquid under IC chips

Prebake ovens can be used to heat the entire motherboard. These are professional grade machines that can be costly. There is a cheaper way to achieve the same results, which is to use the heat gun to heat the motherboard, ensuring that you cover any exposed plastic ports or parts. You will be holding the heat gun 4 to 6 inches away from the motherboard and then heating the entire board both top and bottom sides. You will bring the board to a temperature of 140 to 160 degrees Celsius. It would be impossible to get the entire board this even temperature using a heat gun, so concentrate on a 4 inch square area at a time until you have covered the board. Remember to cover all the areas of the motherboard that house components such as the drive bay ports, the ribbon cable ports, the CMOS battery, the RAM ports and so on. When going over the motherboard, you will concentrate the heating on the IC chips of the board, you must be sure to not overheat the board, use a thermometer when heating.

A Laptops Southbridge, Northbridge and GPU/CPU Chipsets

A laptops Southbridge, Northbridge and GPU/CPU Chipsets; Chip integration, about the chipsets:

About the Integrated and connected ICs

With the progression of technology, manufacturers have designed integrated ICs to allow smaller laptop designs. In the Laptops Today, the IC Chipsets will be combined into one chip instead of having to use separate chips for each. You will see the Southbridge integrated with the GPU (video), you will also see the Northbridge integrated with the GPU, they also have integrated GPU, CPU and Southbridge, and they will have integrated CPU, GPU and Northbridge. As long as these chipsets can receive the proper thermal control, they will run just as if being separate components.

Typically when a Laptop starts to experience video/GPU-BGA failure, it will also show other symptoms such as Missing hard drive, or missing wireless device or missing DVD drive or similar. The reason these other symptoms and secondary failures occur is because of the chip integration. When the video fails, it can affect the Southbridge or the Northbridge and cause these secondary affects to occur.

Cleaning the Laptop and Its Importance

Cleaning the Laptop and Its Importance;

Cleaning the Laptop – Steps Taken, Materials Used

Cleaning tools and materials to be used:

1. Paper Towels

2. Toothbrush

3. Electronic Circuit Board Cleaning Solution

4. Antibacterial Handy-Wipes

5.	Windex Glass Cleaner or Wipes

6.	Compressed Air (not a necessity)

7.	WD-40 Electrical Part Lubricant

Proper Screen Cleaning Method

Cleaning the screen is fairly simple, you can clean it whether it is attached or disassembled. To clean the screens back cover, you will use a basic streak free window cleaner or glass cleaning solution. If there are stickers that need removing, you can spray some WD-40 on the sticker, and let it soak in for a minute or two, then take a guitar pick or similar and gently scrape off the sticker… If you go slow, and don't apply too much pressure, you can remove the majority of the sticker without scratching the cover. Once the majority of the sticker is removed, wipe the area with a dry cloth or paper towel, then re-soak the area with WD-40… now you will use the paper towel to wipe the remaining sticky residue from the cover.

For the screen itself, whether it is a Glossy or Matte Finish, you are to use Streak Free Glass cleaner… I personally use the Windex Handy-Wipes to clean with… Then quickly use a dry clean paper towel to dry the screen… It is very important to dry it very quickly before streaking occurs. It also matters the type of paper towel you use, there are paper towels that are "crispy" and "rough" and can potentially put fine scratches in the screen… then there are Softer paper towels that are practically lint free… This is the kind you will want to use when cleaning the laptop.

Cleaning the Inside of the Laptop

Cleaning of the Fan and Heatsink assembly. Remove the fan/heatsink if you haven't already, making sure that you unplug the fan first.

You will now look on the fan for the retaining screws… You will need a Micro Philips head screwdriver for disassembly of the fan. There are typically 4 screws holding the metal plate onto the fan… Sometimes the screws are hidden under stickers or plastics, and sometimes Rivets are used instead of screws…

If Rivets are used, you will then gently POP the rivet(s). Be as careful as you can not to bend the thin metal fan cover, and if you do bend it, make sure you reshape it back to its original state…

Note that some will use metal/tin rivets and others use plastic rivets… Both are easily broken, and you simply use tape to reseal… NOT Scotch tape… Use a copper foil tape if available, or use thin pieces of electrical tape.

Use the toothbrush to brush out the inside of the bottom base paying extra attention to the fan input and export slots-grates…Then use the toothbrush to clean out the Ethernet port, the audio headphone ports, the VGA port and so on…

Now, back to disassembling the fan and heatsink assembly to clean it…

You first remove the metal shield as discussed earlier... you will now have the fan blade wheel exposed... On most model laptops... they use magnetic oil-less fans...

And they are removable... all you do is grab the fan at both sides (not top and bottom, rather the left and right side)... and wiggle slightly while pulling the fan upward and off the Balancing post that it sits on....

You can now thoroughly clean the fan blades... I will use a damp cleaning cloth when cleaning the blades... It is a good idea to do so because it will remove any sticky residue or remaining dust to give the blades a fresh clean surface for best airflow.

If the fan was making noise before disassembly, you can correct this by using electronic component spray, or wd40... You will have to put the Long Straw attachment onto the spray can, and squirt a small (hardly any) amount into the hole that the fan goes into, also spray the pin on the underside of the fan. You are to use an extremely small amount of this because you just want a light coating on area, you do not want it to puddle or leak onto anywhere else... if too much is applied, it will spread around everywhere once the fan is powered on... and you do not want this to happen.... But once done spraying, quickly take a paper towel piece or similar and try to wipe away any spray that didn't hit the target area...   Then place fan back onto the motor/fan base assembly. Reassemble fan metal shield/Heatsink back together.

Now that you have the keyboard and fan/heatsink cleaned and set aside... Use a toothbrush to carefully clean out the bottom base paying close attention to cleaning the Fan Input and exhaust ports... Then Finish with a cloth/paper towel. I will usually use an antibacterial wipe (wrung out), or a slightly damp paper towel for finishing all the laptops plastic parts.

Cleaning the motherboard is fairly simple. You will use your soft bristled toothbrush to very gently brush over the entire motherboard... Do not apply pressure, as you are only trying to remove any dust that has accumulated. You won't pull off any components if you go slow and brush lightly...

Cleaning the Outside of the Laptop

Window Cleaning solution will suffice for the cleaning of the outside of the laptop, the cover or the rear side of the screen, will usually have scuff marks and light scratches from normal usage. You can use polishes on the back cover, but I don't recommend it. Polishes can leave a film that will attract particles and debris; it can also create static build-up which can be damaging to the Laptop. Using WD-40 or any Electronic lubricant will put a nice shine on the finish, but you must remove it afterwards and only wipe a small amount on, as if it is applied heavily, it will deteriorate the paint resins.

Cleaning the Keyboard

When cleaning the laptop, it is best to first completely disassemble the laptop and arrange your parts on the area near you.

You will start by cleaning the keyboard… I do not recommend using compressed air on the keyboard as it can leave a residue and potentially cause damage to the keyboard.

Using the toothbrush will reach underneath the individual keys, and is abrasive enough to pull any stuck on particles from the key caps without damaging the key itself. Then blow away the debris, and repeat as necessary until clean.

Cleaning the Optical Drives Optical Lens (CD/DVD)

To clean the optical lens, you can do it manually, or you can purchase a cleaning kit. The cleaning kit will usually consist of a cleaning cd, a felt pad or cloth, and a cleaning solution. You simply apply the cleaning solution, spread it around the disc, and insert it to spin and clean the lens.

You can eject the cd/dvd disc tray to gain access to the optical drive on most Laptop optical drives. The optical lens is the part with the eye lens and it is kind of hard to miss. You will use a Qtip or similar to clean the lens, and denatured alcohol or glass cleaning solution (must be streak free), going over the lens once with a damp tip, then another with a dry clean swab to polish the lens.

Make sure to clean the disc tray and surrounding parts and components too, it will allow the disc to spin better.

Some Optical drives will have all the components including the optical lens located in the housing of the drive and will require disassembly. To do this manually, you will need to remove the Optical Drive from the laptop, it is usually secured by one screw on the bottom side of the laptop and towards the middle or center of the laptop, there will be an imprinted icon indicating its location. Remove the securing screw and slide the optical drive out and away from the laptop. You will now need to disassemble the cover of the drive to gain access to the internal components.

The Laptops BIOS

The Laptops BIOS; Editing the settings:

Flashing the BIOS, Editing, Updating and Troubleshooting

Flashing the BIOS can be done by browsing to the website of the Laptops manufacturer. From the websites main page, you will be looking for the Service and Support section and from the sub category, you will be choosing, downloads and drivers or similar. You will be prompted to either choose or enter the model number or service tag number of that Laptop in question, once entered; you will be taken to the Drivers page where you select the Operating System currently installed on that machine. You will then scroll down to BIOS update download, and you simply click the download link and Save it or Run it.

You must make sure that you have the battery inserted and the AC Adapter plugged in when attempting to update your BIOS, this is a fail-safe feature to ensure the download and install complete without a glitch. If anything were to mess up the install during the middle of that install, it could render the

Laptop Useless, Needing to ReFlash the BIOS Chip, or Replacing the Motherboard to Correct the BIOS failure issue. Troubleshooting can be done from certain BIOS utility screens, and you are allowed to run tests on the RAM, Graphics and Hard Drive. This feature is usually located in the Advanced or Troubleshooting section of the BIOS.

The Tools Used To Repair Laptops

The Tools Used To Repair Laptops;   **Hand Tools and Power Tools:**

Hand Tools Used

Screwdriver: you will need both micro sized screwdrivers and medium sized ones, it is best to find a variety pack so that you will get ones with different shaped tips, being narrow ones and blunt ones.

Pliers: the needle-nosed pliers are the most used, and not the typical thick ones available, you will need to search out thin and narrow ones, the smaller the better as you will need to use these pliers in very tight spaces and picking up very small items.

Desoldering Tool Set: This can be found in most electronics stores, and is sold in a set; you will get metal picks, plastic picks, scraping wands, metal brushes and so on…

Wrenches: It is good to have a variety of sized wrenches, though you will find yourself using the needle-nosed pliers in the wrenches place

Plastic Pry Tools: This will include guitar picks, plastic wand style pry tool (like the ones given with iPod repair part purchases), thin plastic cards and similar

Star Tip Screwdriver inserts: These are needed quite often in case disassembly, especially on Mac based machines, you will need to get a variety pack with these due to the many size screws used.

Allen Wrenches: Not so commonly used but they are used and if you repair Laptops on a regular basis, you will come across a repair needing an Allen wrench, it is best to get a variety pack here too, though it is usually sold as a set.

Razor Knife: Used to strip wires, cut tape, pry components and many other uses.

Toothbrush: Used quite often, it will allow the removal of dust and debris without harming the components.

Earth Magnet: These magnets can be bought from your local electronics store and will be a lot stronger than the typical magnet. They are used to magnetize your tools, and small enough to keep attached to a screwdriver or similar.

Lighted Magnifying Glass: Get the best you can find here, a headset will work good, you want one that will allow you to stay hands-free.

Power Tools Used

Soldering Gun: You will use what you are comfortable here with, wand style, the gun style, or the station style. If your budget allows, you should get a soldering or rework station.

Heat Gun/Hot Air gun: This will be used in the reflow process for the video chip connection. You can purchase these at any Home Improvement store all over the world, they are typically used in the Painting field, they are used to strip paint. In Electronics repair they are used as well, just not advertised as such. You will need on that can reach solder melting point temperatures. The 2 setting (high-low) Heat guns will suffice, though I do recommend the multi setting 600 to 1200 watt heat gun, set to 700-800 on the heat dial.

Thermometer: The recommended thermometer is an infrared laser guided digital thermometer; you must ensure that it can read temperatures past 223 degrees Celsius and 433 degrees Fahrenheit.

All Battery Operated Testing Tools: Multimeter, Oscilloscope, Capacitance Meter, Continuity Tester

Dremel Tool: This is a micro sized multipurpose drill and will come in handy for multiple jobs.

Air Compressor: This would be used if you have professional tools. Some soldering stations and rework stations will use forced air, they connect to an air compressor.

Electronic Testing Equipment Used

OHMMETER: Used for measuring insulation-resistance or other high electrical resistances

CAPACITANCE METER: Used to test ceramic and electrolytic capacitors for faulty components or beginning stages of failure and loss of function to that component.

MULTIMETER: Used for a wide variety of testing, mainly, it will be used for ad/dc testing of components on the laptop. DC Jack and AC Adapter testing is a common use for the multimeter.

CIRCUIT CONTINUITY TESTER: Used to test for breaks or shorts in plugs, wires and traces.

OSCILLOSCOPE: An oscilloscope is a test instrument which allows you to look at the 'shape' of electrical signals by displaying a graph of voltage against time on its screen. It is like a voltmeter with the valuable extra function of showing how the voltage varies with time.

DIGITAL INFRARED THERMOMETER: Used in laptop repairing for temperature measurement from a distance without contact with the object to be measured.

Integrated/Onboard Video Chip (GPU) Repair

Integrated/Onboard Video Chip (GPU) Repair; Graphics/Video/GPU can fail due to Thermal Damage:

Laptops and Notebooks have either integrated (Onboard) video, or, they use a video card. About 80% of today's Laptops use Integrated Graphics Chips.

About the BGA

The BGA is descended from the pin grid array (PGA), which is a package with one face covered (or partly covered) with pins in a grid pattern. These pins conduct electrical signals from the integrated circuit to the printed circuit board (PCB) on which it is placed. In a BGA, the pins are replaced by balls of solder stuck to the bottom of the package. These solder spheres can be placed manually or with automated equipment. The solder spheres are held in place with a tacky flux until soldering occurs. [1] The device is placed on a PCB that carries copper pads in a pattern that matches the solder balls. The assembly is then heated, either in a reflow oven or by an infrared heater, causing the solder balls to melt. Surface tension causes the molten solder to hold the package in alignment with the circuit board, at the correct separation distance, while the solder cools and solidifies.

Reflowing the GPU

Video Failure Repairing, Video Chip/GPU/Graphics Chip Reflow-Repair Method

Do It Yourself Video Chip BGA Rework (Reflow)

Understanding the GPU, CPU, Memory Chips and Ball Grid Arrays (BGA's):

Q: What are these chip packages that Microsoft® calls the GPU, the CPU, and the Memory Chips?

And why do they look so different from other components?

A: These are electronic chips that are packaged in what are called Ball Grid Array formats (BGA's).

They are a relatively new form of Surface Mount Devices (SMD) and are similar to other components in that they have an integrated circuit (die) within the package and that they have connections to be Soldered. However, instead of leads at the side of the chip, the connections are balls underneath the chip):

Faulty NVidia Chip...Both Intel and AMD Based Motherboards...Though More Common on the AMD...

The symptoms of the Laptop Powering on and shutting off repeatedly...Or... Powering On and Having No Video...

Or... Power Strip Lights Up, Beeps, Shuts Down...Or...No Power At All...Or... Intermittent Loss Of Wireless/Video Goes In And Out/Touchpad Slows and Freezes...

Next step Is preparing the Motherboard...you need to Insulate all areas around the Video Chip/GPU...This is where you will use the Tin Foil...make sure to Use About 4 Fold Thickness (fold the aluminum foil 4 times to make it thicker).. And Place Foil Over The CPU, Over Any Plastic Plug Ports... Over Any Capacitors Nearby...

It Is Important To Clear Your Work Area Now... You Will Be Working with A lot Of Heat and anything around will Get Real Hot

I Use Metal And Aluminum Foil, I also Work On A Marble Table, You Will Want To Make Sure That You Have Foil Or Non-Flammable Surface Under The Motherboard. The More You Cover... The Better

Now It's Time To Weight The Chip...This Serves 2 Purposes...

1.)	Most Graphics Chips Have An Epoxy That Goes Around The Edge Of The Chip To Hold It In Its Position And To Prevent Chip Rising and I explain in this book How to remove it safely...The Weight of the Coin Stack Helps To Get A Better Reflow...Don't Worry, It's Not Enough Weight To Squish The Chip Into The Board.. Through Trial And Error, I've Determined That 6 Quarters and 2 Nickels Is the Proper Weight for an NVidia Chip...Use Less Weight for a Smaller Chip.

2.)	The Stack of Quarters Also Helps to Spread the Heat More evenly and Helps Prevent the Upper Chip That Rests on the Video Chip from Overheating

Different Ways to Heat the Chip:

Rework Stations are common to Reflowing and Reballing IC Chipsets, They are machines that will brace the motherboard, allow for proper heating of the board before reflowing, to prevent board shock, they can concentrate the high heat to center on the IC chip needed to be reflowed without overheating other components… There are Hot Air Rework Stations, and there are Infrared Rework Stations… IR stations will heat the board using light… and can be known for yielding better results because the heat can be concentrated on the specific area without heating surrounding components.

You will be using Hot Air for your repairing… There are a lot of skeptics out there claiming that hot air methods Do Not work. This misinformation is wrong….In my opinion, it is a better option, specifically referring to the Use of a Hot Air Heat Gun. Reason being, you are able to maneuver the source of heat, and manipulate the Flow of heat by the use of Heat Gun Add-On Tips.

These add-on tips are extremely useful… You can purchase the exact tip needed to fit exactly over the chip needed to be reflowed… there are many different styles available.

Free movement of the heat source allows you to angle the hot air flow to reach under the chips edge better…You can adjust the Heat temperature on most Heat Guns..

You can also Use the 2 setting Heat guns, but you should practice Chip heating on a Non-Working motherboard to get used to the time length of chip heating.

Using a Hot Air gun together with an Infrared Digital Thermometer will yield just as accurate if not, more accurate results when reflowing (not referring to Reballing here), because you have the ability to angle the heat source, and the ability to circulate the edge of the chip in a clockwise motion. Once you begin heating any motherboard, it is important to keep it Level and Stable.

Using the infrared Thermometer will take you a little bit of practice, as if it is used wrong it will yield misleading results… which could end up in overheating the Chipset if not getting the correct readings.

These Infrared thermometers are laser guided… You simply point the red dot to the spot you are testing for temperature readings. You should be holding the gun at a 45 degree angle and about 4 to 6 inches from the chip to get the correct readings… You do not exceed 223 degrees Celsius for the GPU heating.

Now Comes the Heating of the Chip

Turn Your Heat Gun On Low…

Start at about 4 inches From the Chip…

You want to be holding the gun at a 45% angle…

Aim the heat at the Edge of the chip, You Will Start Rotating around the Chip- around the outer edge of the chip…then use tighter circles concentrating on the quarter stack, then after about 30-40 seconds, slowly move closer to the chip…You Want to Heat the Chip slowly… This Will At The Same Time Pre-Bake The Underside Of The Board…

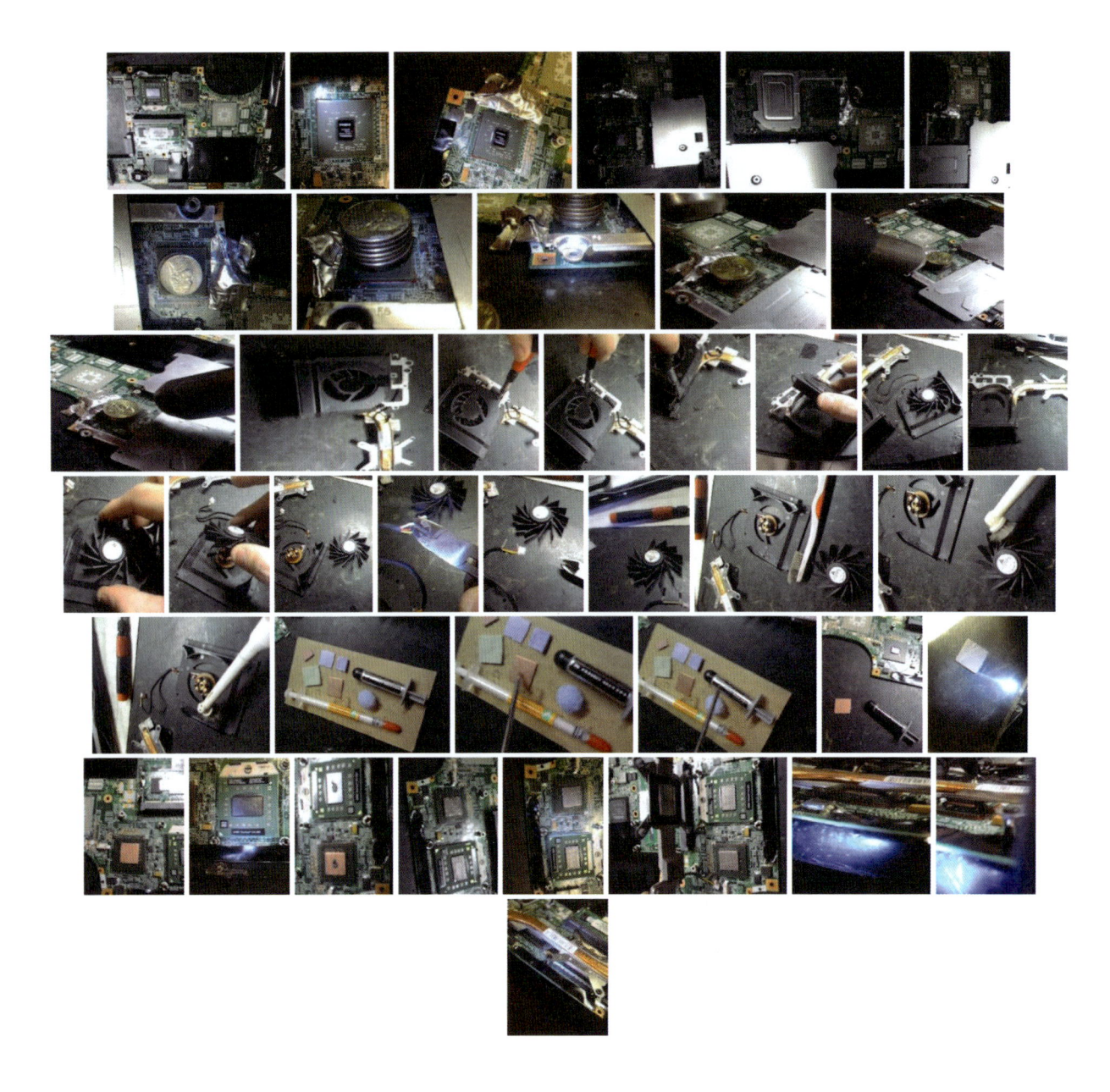

Never Move the Heat Gun Closer than the Top Of Your Coin Stack...Then Pull It Back And Slowly Repeat... The Chip Needs To Get Hot Enough

To Re-Melt the Solder Balls on the underside of the graphics chip back down to the contact pads on the Motherboard... and this takes Quite

A lot of heating to do.... You Must Not OVERHEAT the Chip... It Is Best To Under heat it and have to Redo... than to overheat... It will cause

The solder to break down and even crack/split... causing failure forever...

This process will take about 3 minutes total... Once you shut off the Heat Gun... Leave The Stack of Coins on the Chip and Let Sit for another 5 minutes...

It is important to not take the heat above 433 F   or   223 C

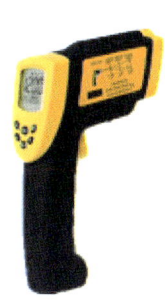

This is where a digital temperature probe comes in handy...If one is available to you, or you can purchase one... You will have better results

Now If you have a lot Of Repair Experience and Are Capable... You Can Go One Step Further And DO A Re-ball... You Would Be Completely Removing The Graphics Chip And Using Solder Wick To Clean The Contact Points On Both The Chip And The Motherboard. If Doing This, I recommend CHIP QUIK SMD REMOVAL KIT

Then Re-Balling Both The Chip And The Motherboard...To Do This, You Need To Add New Solder Balls To Each Contact Pad On The Chip And To The Motherboard.

You Would Also Need To Remove the Epoxy That the Factory Uses To Secure the Chip

The Process Once Again, A Little More Detailed...

And now it is time to start your heat gun... You should be using 600 to 800 degrees Fahrenheit temperature... Or if you have a 2 setting heat gun, then use the LOW setting...

Now you will add a Coin Stack to the top of the GPU on the Video Card... You will be Using 6 Quarters, And 2 Nickels

All U.S. nickels weigh 5 gm.

A Modern copper-nickel quarter dated 1965 and later will weigh 5.67 grams

You Place the 2 Nickels On the Chip First... This is because the Nickel is closer to the same size as the upper chip, being that the quarters are larger and higher up from the chips surface, will help pull the Heat away quicker and will heat the chip more thoroughly...

And now comes the Reflowing of the BGA GPU. If you don't have use of an infrared thermometer, you will have to judge your reflow by length of time...

Starting Your Reflow...

You start By Aiming your Heat Gun and turning it on, Hold at 45 degree angle, it's a Good Idea to Use a Stopwatch too... Type: STOPWATCH into Google and Run a Free One On Your Screen While Reflowing...

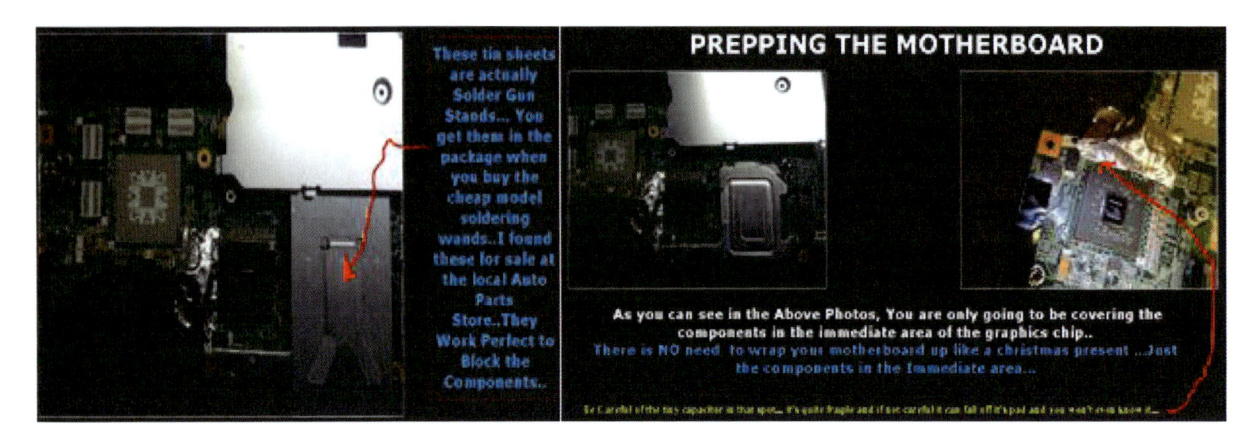

OK, As Soon as You Start Heating the Chip, You Will Be Aiming the Heat Gun around the Outer Edge of the Chip-.And The Base of the Coin Stack....

At The 1 Minute Point of Heating... Look At Your Digital Thermometer... You Should Be At A Temperature Of 160 Degrees Celsius...Then At The 2 minute point of reflowing... you should be at a temperature of 195 degrees Celsius....Then... at around 2:45 or 3 minutes... you should reach 223 degrees Celsius... the Reflow Point... The Point at Which The BGA Solder Turns To A Liquid State... And The Cracks/Faults In the Cold Solder BGA Should Reconnect/Recorrect.... In Turn, Repairing the Chip...

Once you have reached the correct temperature or time length... let the coin stack sit on top of the chip until cooled... then remove the coin stack and tin sheets/foil...

Now, when applying silver paste to the chip, you do not put a "ton" of it on... You will apply a thin layer of paste to the chip, and then, most importantly, you will then smooth the paste onto the chip... you spread it like making a peanut butter and jelly sandwich... make it Smooth! You don't want pits and dips in the paste... you want it looking like a Frosted Cake...

If your GPU had a thermal pad and didn't originally have thermal paste on it... then you will use a thermal pad again... whether it is the same pad as originally used, or a NEW replacement pad...It is important that a pad is used to allow for natural expansion/contraction of the fragile upper "flip" chip of the GPU..

And now you will put the Heatsink/Fan Assembly back onto the video chip/GPU or card.

Make sure to plug the fan back into its port on the card.

Now you are ready to test the card.

Removing the Chip Sealant

HOW TO REMOVE THE RED (or clear) GPU/GRAPHICS CHIP SEALANT SAFELY FROM THE CHIPS OUTER EDGE:

You will need to prepare the board, covering any plastic parts, covering RAM ports, Covering CPU Base, etc....

Then Heat the Chips outer edge using The Heat Gun at 700 Degrees, Monitor the temperature with the infrared thermometer and bring the chips outer edge to a temperature of 145 degrees Celsius...

It would be a good idea to practice removal on a "dead" motherboard before attempting on the board you are repairing, unless you are familiar with the process and have done it more than a couple times...

Main thing here is to go slow and do not overheat the chip doing it... Heat one side at a time... then gently scrape that one side... then heat the next side, then scrape and so on…

The Coin Stack – Used in the Reflow Process, A KEY INSTRUMENT IN VIDEO CHIP REPAIR

This is the key to a successful reflow, and the reason for my patent and trademark...

The coin stack plays several roles in the Reflow process... And Is the Reason why My Method Works and the "viral" YouTube Videos Do not...

I use a Coin stack because of the availability of a Coin world-wide... I started Out before Releasing this Method Using a Block of Silver, which equaled the weight of 6 Quarters and 2 Nickels... And since coins are easy for everyone World-Wide to obtain... I went with the common choice...

The Metal Compounds that make up these 2 coins will help greatly in the Dissipation of Heat.

The Importance of weighting the chip is my other main key reason for this method and its success...

It's a matter of the Laws of Science that anything being heated...especially to the temperature of a reflow.... will want to expand (as opposed to contracting)... and by nature... the chip will want to "expand" and rise up from its connection... This is also why Chip Sealant is used by the manufacturers...

So when heating the chip for a Reflow... Weighting this GPU chip will help to prevent chip rising and popcorning... Makes Sense Right?? Say "yes"....Cause It does... I have done extensive testing on this by using various weights and temperatures...

Now... the other purpose the coinstack serves is... It Protects the Chip

It protects it by covering the "flip chip" or Upper Chip... This is extremely important and was completely overlooked in any other Reflow process method I've come across...

The reason this is important is that when heating the graphics chip either in a Rework Station or by using a Heat gun... This Smaller Chip Is The First Chip Being Exposed to The High Heat... And Being that it is a Smaller and Thinner chip... It is going to heat up to the point of reflow Way before the Lower Larger Chip Reaches the Proper Reflow Temperature...So that if No coin stack is used the Fully Exposed chip can possibly be irreversibly damaged before the lower chip reflow is complete...

The Coin Stack Prevents this from happening by its ability to Dissipate the heat rapidly from that upper chip during the heating process and not allowing direct heat to make contact ... Though this Flip Chip is allowed to still reach Reflow temperature at the same time as the Lower chip, Or not at all if desired... it is completely controllable now...The Coins will also Help In the Cooling Process, as they Will Pull the Heat from The Chip Much Quicker And Directly Instead of Dispersing it Downward through the Motherboard, which is Extremely Important.

External Video/GPU Card Repair

External Video/GPU Card Repair;   **Video cards are common in laptops and are removable:**

Repairing the Laptops Video Card, Repairing the Desktops Video Card

REPAIRING A DESKTOP COMPUTER's VIDEO CARD

You Will Be Reflowing the GPU on the Card's board, The Repair Method Can Be Applied to ANY Video Card

This Video Card happened to have a "clean" fan... Most will be loaded with dust and debris and will need to be cleaned before repair completion.

Start the Repair by Unplugging the Fan/Heatsink Assembly from the Board...

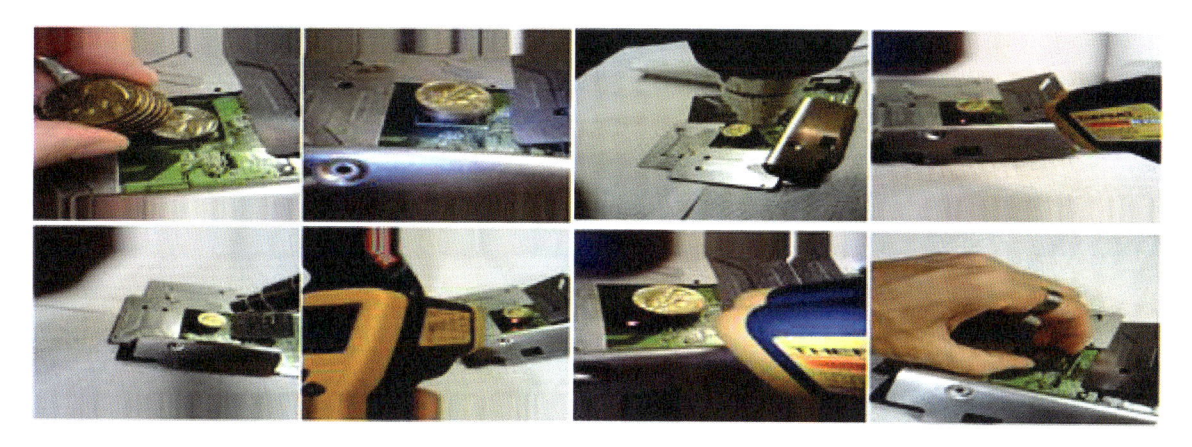

Desktop Video Card Failure is an extremely common issue, to which the only "fix" has been to Throw out the card and replace it with a new one...

Cards today can be quite costly...Costing up to $700.00(USD) and Higher...and to simply replace that expensive card is not an option for some people, and can render the computer Non-Working...

Most video card Failure Issues ARE related to Thermal Breakdown

A Desktop Video Card Has a Heat Sink and Fan for a Reason...it covers the GPU or Graphics /Video Chip to keep it cool. The GPU can fail when over exposed to extreme heat and internal case temperatures. The failure is usually due to the fan/heatsink assembly becoming clogged and hindering the full capability of the fan which in turn can cause faults in the BGA of the Graphics chip, causing the card to Not work, which causes the Desktop to Not Work and Not Able to POST.

The Same Method That Applies to Laptop Video Chip Repair, Applies also to Desktop Video Cards

Step 1 is to remove the Fan, Heatsink Assembly from the Video Card. To do this, you need to turn the video card to the opposite side of the fan (on most cards), and look for the Pin Clamps or Spring Screws... In the photos, the Plastic pop-thru and Lock type is used, and to remove, you will need to use a pair of needle nosed pliers and squeeze the 2 prongs together to be able to push the pins back through the holes...

Pull the Fan/Heatsink Assembly away from the video card and Set Aside.

At this time, you should Clean the Fan Blades, and the heatsink, Remove the Crusty Old Silver Thermal Paste and Replace with a SMOOTH Layer of New Silver Thermal Paste...

Next, it's time to Insulate the surrounding components on the video card to keep them cool during the reflow process... It is not necessary to Completely Wrap the card like a Christmas present with tin foil...

And now it is time to start your heat gun... You should be using 600 to 800 degrees Fahrenheit temperature... Or if you have a 2 setting heat gun, then use the LOW setting...

Now you will add a Coin Stack to the top of the GPU on the Video Card... You will be Using 6 Quarters, And 2 Nickels

All U.S. nickels weigh 5 gm.

A Modern copper-nickel quarter dated 1965 and later will weigh 5.67 grams

You Place the 2 Nickels On the Chip First... This is because the Nickel is closer to the same size as the upper chip, being that the quarters are larger and higher up from the chips surface, will help pull the Heat away quicker and will heat the chip more thoroughly...

And now comes the Reflowing of the BGA GPU. If you don't have use of an infrared thermometer, you will have to judge your reflow by length of time...

Starting Your Reflow...

You start By Aiming your Heat Gun and turning it on, Hold at 45 degree angle, it's a Good Idea to Use a Stopwatch too... Type: STOPWATCH into Google and Run a Free One On Your Screen While Reflowing...

OK, As Soon as You Start Heating the Chip, You Will Be Aiming the Heat Gun around the Outer Edge of the Chip-.And The Base of the Coin Stack....

At The 1 Minute Point of Heating... Look At Your Digital Thermometer... You Should Be At A Temperature Of 160 Degrees Celsius...Then At The 2 minute point of reflowing... you should be at a temperature of 195 degrees Celsius....Then... at around 2:45 or 3 minutes... you should reach 223 degrees Celsius... the Reflow Point... The Point at Which The BGA Solder Turns To A Liquid State... And The Cracks/Faults In the Cold Solder BGA Should Reconnect/Recorrect.... In Turn, Repairing the Chip...

Once you have reached the correct temperature or time length... let the coin stack sit on top of the chip until cooled... then remove the coin stack and tin sheets/foil...

Now.... When applying silver paste to the chip, you do not put a "ton" of it on... You will apply a thin layer of paste to the chip, and then, most importantly, you will then smooth the paste onto the chip... you spread it like making a peanut butter and jelly sandwich... make it Smooth! You don't want pits and dips in the paste... you want it looking like a Frosted Cake... If your GPU had a thermal pad and didn't originally have thermal paste on it... then you will use a thermal pad again... whether it is the same pad as originally used, or a NEW replacement pad...It is important that a pad is used to allow for natural expansion/contraction of the fragile upper "flip" chip of the GPU..

And now you will put the Heatsink/Fan Assembly back onto the video card.

Make sure to plug the fan back into its port on the card. Now you are ready to test the card.

Laptop Case Disassembly

Laptop Case Disassembly;   A General Guideline and Summary to Disassembling Any Laptop:

There is a Method to a Laptop Breakdown, Case Removal, Which will apply to any Make or Model Laptop or Notebook, I will explain....

When disassembling any laptop, always start from the bottom of the laptop. Start by removing all visible screws from the laptops underside, I will always start from the rear side of the bottom of the laptop, then, I will move to the Battery Bay to remove the screws in there.   Next, always look at the back of the laptop for screws.. With the lid closed, look near the Hinge cover areas, and below the hinge covers... Usually 1 or 2 screws are used in those areas... It's ok if you don't find any too, a lot of laptops don't use any screws there...

   Notice on the under-side (bottom) of the laptop that there are Icons next to some of the screw holes. Some laptops will put imprinted Icons next to the screw holes that connect to components of the laptop, like the keyboard, which will show a keyboard icon. The CDrom will show a CD icon, and the Ram Port Cover will show a memory stick icon.

A laptop will typically use 2 to 4 different screw sizes or types... and they will repeat use through the whole laptop – inside and out. Over time, you will familiarize yourself with the placement of the different sizes and the reasoning for each size. For instance.. Inside the battery bay, you will usually find 2 or more screws there that secure the media strip on the palmrest to the bottom base... and these are always small/short screws. Then you have the screws that are located on the bottom rear of every laptop that secure the hinges to the bottom base. These screws are always longer... Then if shorter ones are used again, they would be found in areas like... under the keyboard, in the hard drive bay(s), in the cd/dvd drive bay, and so on... The Screen area is the same way... Longer screws are used at the bottom (thicker) area... then at the top of the screen area, the smaller/shorter screws are used...

Be very careful when disassembling the laptop to make note and remember which sizes go where, because if you use a long screw where a short one should go, you can cause damage to parts on/in the laptop. For instance, If you are reassembling and have the screen attached and are now attaching the palmrest to the bottom base, and you put a screw that is too long into the front bottom of the laptop, It will poke through the plastic palmrest and either leave a permanent Bump in the plastic, or it will pierce the plastic and create a Hole. Same goes for any other area, you can potentially Short out the motherboard if the wrong screw is used. So Be Careful in this area... Take Photos of your disassembly if needed to learn the proper placement. When in doubt, go with a smaller/shorter screw...

Disassembly of the laptop is done the same way for all models..

First, The Bottom base has all screws removed.

Next, the hard drive, the Wi-Fi Card(s) the battery, the RAM, and the CD/DVD drive are removed.

Note that the CD rom always has at least 1 screw securing it to the laptop located at the rear end of where it sits in the laptop, accessible from the bottom side, near the center. The Hard drive will have 2, 3 or 4 screws securing it, and these screws are typically thicker than any other screw used on that laptop. Some Hard Drives will slide in and out of a Slot Port, which are usually located on the side of the laptop. And Some Hard Drives will be connected using a ribbon cable, some will plug in and some will slide in. Usually if you see a Pull Tab on the hard drive, you pull upward or backward depending on the port connection type.

Once all screws are removed from the bottom side of the bottom base, you then look at the rear of the laptop (the back where all ports and connections are located), and look near the Hinge and Hinge cover area for any screws, as there are sometimes 1 or 2 on each side to be removed.

Now, concentrate on the palmrest and keyboard removal. Starting by Removing the keyboard..

With some (actually most) laptops, there will be a media strip cover that is located just above the keyboard on the palmrest/bottom base upper half. This is snapped down, as well as secured by those small screws in the battery bay as described earlier... You will use a thin plastic tool (like a guitar pick) to pry the plastic strip from the base. Before doing this, look to see if there is a secondary plastic keyboard upper screw cover strip to be removed, this is common on Toshiba models... and will need to be removed prior to removing the media strip. To remove the media strip you begin at one of the side edges, prying upward until it unsnaps. Some models are harder to start on the side edge and in this case, you will go to the center area and stick your plastic pry tool in one of the keyboard screw flattened areas... You can see the metal keyboard base tray has flattened areas (3 or 4 usually) along the top and that area leaves a gap between the plastic media strip and the keyboard... in the center area... and this is where you will pry in an upward motion to unsnap the plastic strip from the bottom base/palmrest. Once you have it started, you continue around the whole strip unsnapping the whole panel.. Be Very careful here, because a lot of laptop models have these media strips with lights/buttons/controllers attached to them, and will have short wire or ribbon cable connections going from them to the motherboard... And If You Pry upward and pull the media strip away too fast or too much/ too far, you can damage these fragile ribbon cables and wires... The best way to do it is to gently unsnap the plastic strip so it is free from the bottom base, then tip it towards yourself pulling the top upward towards you...it will reveal any connected wires or cables and you can safely remove or unattach them at this time..

Let me note here the common connections of cables...

RIBBON STYLE CABLES

Ribbon cables will connect to a Slot style port, the cables plug end will lock down, and there are 2 common types of port lock tabs.

FLIP DOWN style, which has a plastic flap that flips up to unlock and flips down to lock, you can use a guitar pick to pry the flap upward to unlock it and release the ribbon cable..

The second style uses two locking plastic tabs on either side of the port, the tabs are slid upward (not up toward you, rather, up toward the screen). Unlock both sides, only sliding them upward a few millimeters... do not pull too hard or they will break or pop off... If this happens... try to resnap them back in/on...

This will also apply to The Keyboard Connection, as It Typically Uses a Ribbon Cable Connection... Though On Some Models... the ribbon cable will have a convenient Plug end on the end of the cable so all you do is pull on the attached wire bar or sticker on the plug end and pull upward towards yourself.. No Unlocking or Unsnapping to do here...

Now comes the Removal of the Keyboard and any Hinge covers that are still attached.

To start the keyboard removal, you will first look at the top of the keyboard for securing screws. If there are any, remove them (typically 2 to 4 are used). Now you will grab ahold of the top area of the keyboard on both left and right sides and attempt to pull upward toward yourself. If it does not lift upward easily, you might have the type that have a slot style connection Planer Board located at the bottom middle of the keyboard... these type will slide upward to be removed, Once you slide it upward toward the screen, you pull Upward toward yourself to release the keyboard.. On all other models you continue pulling upward and flip it over laying it face down on the touchpad area, this will allow you to easily have access to the ribbon cable port that connects the keyboard to the motherboard...

If for some reason, you try removing the keyboard pulling it upward/outward and it is stuck, you need to flip the laptop over and re-check to ensure all keyboard securing screws were removed and none remain... they are usually labeled with a stamped plastic Keyboard Icon imprinted right into the plastic in the areas that have keyboard screws..

Note here that some models like Compaq, will use a plastic trim piece that surrounds the keyboard, it is snapped on as well and you will use a guitar pick to remove this.

Remove keyboard and set aside. You will now/should now be able to remove the screen...

All screens have wires and or cables that go from the screen down into the bottom base to connect to the motherboard... And they almost always will travel down through the hinge area...

You will now need to unplug and unattach any and all cables coming from the screen... Then you can unscrew the screen at the Hinge posts to free it from the bottom base. Then Pull it upward and away from the laptop and set aside... At this point you will be removing any and all visible screws from the palmrest area... including where the keyboard once sat...

Now you will need to remove the palmrest from the lower base... It is attached by snap tabs, you again need a guitar pick or similar, start at the front corner and pry the palmrest upward to unsnap it...

Some laptop models will have a plastic molding strip at the rear of the palmrest/base that is only accessible once the screen is removed, models like the HP dv series Will have these, and they are secured by 1 screw and then snapped down, you will remove the retaining screw and use plastic pry tool to pry upward and inward to unsnap it and release it.

You hopefully now will have the screen, the keyboard, the palmrest and all plastics removed and set aside... Now the Motherboard should be exposed and you're almost done with the disassembly...

NOTE that Tablet style will differ slightly in disassembly and wire/plug locations will also differ.

Another thing to note is that there are a few models out there that are the exact opposite and actually have the motherboard attached to the palmrest and the first piece to be removed is the underside or Bottom Base... Sony VAIO is a good example of a manufacturer that uses this style...

Now, to remove the motherboard from the bottom base...

Most motherboards, including real old models, will have numbers or some kind of sign, like an arrow next to the screws that are securing the motherboard to the base... If that is not the case on the board you have, then you will simply remove any and all visible screws. There will also be many plugs and cables still attached to the motherboard, and some need to be unplugged/disconnected, and some don't. You will need to determine that by physically inspecting both ends of the cable in question and determining if it's removal is needed to pull the board away from the base…. And do so accordingly. A lot of motherboards will also have secondary boards connected to them, they will connect either by the board plugging into them, or they will plug into the board, or they will connect using a wire or cable. Remove or unattach and set aside. On some models you will need to disconnect the fan and heatsink assembly before removing the motherboard, if so, do so… be careful to unplug the CPU/GPU fan plug as well at this time… Pull the motherboard away from the Bottom Base, You Can leave the DC Jack connected on some models, some models have the dc jack that connects with wire/plug style as opposed to soldered directly to the board.. and with the wire style, some are attached using a locking plug style and some are a permanent plug port that does not unsnap.., then some models, such as HP dv series, have a plug in/out type that you will need to Unplug before removing the motherboard... This is done by raising the area of the motherboard nearest the DC Jack plug port connection, raise the board about an inch and you will have enough access to be able to Pull the plug end downward to unplug it from its port on the underside of the motherboard..

Now Remove the motherboard and set aside...

On the models that still have the heatsink and fan assembly attached, you can go ahead now and remove that too.

That is basically it for laptop disassembly, each model will slightly differ, but following these general rules will get you through any removal or disassembly.

Disassembling the Screen

With all screens, you will start with removing the front frame or bezel, which involves removing the screw covers, removing all screws along the top, sides and bottom. Then you unsnap the bezel and set aside. If a power inverter exists in the housing it will typically be located under the screen display panel and you will want to loosen and remove any screws attaching it to the rear panel. Then proceed to the sides of the screen where the hinge posts secure to the screen. You will remove all screws attaching the screen to the posts (usually 2 to 4 on each side). Proceed to the top of the screen and remove any securing screws holding the screen to the rear panel, also unplug the webcam if one exists. Pulling the screen top half outward towards you, you will lay the screen flat down on top of the palmrest and unstick the display cable securing tape, peeling it downward until you reach the part where the plug is, then you will use the tape as a handle to unplug the screen display cable, leaving the tape/handle attached to the cable. Now you can unplug the power inverter wires from the inverter plug end which will free the screen and you can now remove the display panel and set aside. All that is left in the screen area will be a webcam, possibly the webcam cable, the microphone if one exists, the Wi-Fi cables and antennas, and the hinge posts and bracings.

Removing the screen from the lower base assembly

To remove the whole assembled screen away from the base, you will start by removing any hinge covers or keyboard-media strip to gain access to the hinge post screw location. Typically all hinges will be screwed onto the base using 2 to 4 screws, the usual being 2 per side. There can also be screws that secure from the bottom of the laptop and screws located on the back (rear) of the laptops base. Make sure to unplug all exiting cables

Removing the Palmrest

Some models will not allow the removal of the palmrest because the motherboard is attached to it as its base. Sony Vaio is a typical example of this style, but we will discuss the more common type which has the motherboard's base being the bottom base unit. Most palm rests will be the entire area from the front of the laptop, to the back, and some will be pieced together in sections. ThinkPad's will be in sections, having a front section, a mid-section and a rear section to remove. With all palmrest removals, you will start at the bottom side of the laptop for all makes and models. It will be best just to remove all screws from the underside to save time and frustration. Once all visible screws are removed, then, remove all attached components such as the hard drive(s) and DVD/CD tray and the battery. Look in the empty bays of the components you just removed for any screws and remove them. Certain hard drive bays will have access to small motherboard screws that do not get removed (they are smaller than any case securing screw).

The Hinge Cover

Hinge covers will vary in styles, some will be individual caps that cover each hinge separately and some will be part of the media strip or upper keyboard /power button cover. You will need to make sure there are no screws attaching it to the bare, if so remove them before removing the cap. Any other type will usually unsnap from the base as long as no other parts are covering its locking tabs.

Soldering

Soldering;   Tools and equipment used for laptop soldering:

Soldering gun vs. Soldering wand vs. soldering station

Let's start with the best choice, which is a soldering station or a rework station. There are many varieties and grades of these available. You can get just a soldering gun, or you can get a station that includes a desoldering gun and a vacuum, and blower, and heat gun if chosen. And those choices offer variable quality selections and available features for the higher quality stations like more control over the temperature settings, digital readout and more.

Using the wand style will work just as well, though these are sold in Watts, and if you are doing laptop repair, you will want a 35 watt or greater. If you get a lesser watt one, you will not be able to properly heat the solder quickly and will result in poor quality soldering, or part damage.

I can't speak too much about the gun style soldering gun because I do not like using them. The shape and the way it is held just did not work with me trying to maneuver around the laptop motherboard as it doesn't have the length that is needed, and the tip was too big and too thick for the micro components.

Types of solder to use on Laptop Motherboards

Types of Solder to Use: The solder can be bought or ordered from any Local Home Improvement Store or Hardware Store... Though A Typical Hardware Store Will Not Sell The Correct Type, They Sell Plumbing Solder Usually...

The Solder I find Is Best Is:

62/36/2 ROSIN-CORE SOLDER

.022"-Diameter High Tech Silver-Bearing

Net Wt.: 1.5 oz. (42.5g)

Soldering;   Types of Fluxes and their uses:

Rosin Paste Flux and its use

Rosin fluxes are used for both wave soldering and in solder paste for reflow soldering. Rosin is inactive at room temperature but becomes active when heated to soldering temperatures. The melting point of rosin is 172 to 175) C, or just below the melting point of solder (1830C) which is a desirable property. As the rosin fluxes are weak, halide activators are used. Rosin fluxes can be classified into three groups.

    1. Rosin activated (RA)

    2. Rosin mildly activated (RMA)

    3. Rosin (R)

These three categories differ basically in the concentration of activators. As the name suggests, the cleaning action of RA flux more powerful than RMA flux and also requires through cleaning after reflow. The residue after soldering of RMA flux by itself is not very harmful, it may attract dust and other harmful chemicals from atmosphere and therefore it is recommended to clean the same after reflow. RMA flux is the most common one used for surface mount reflow applications. The rosin fluxes can be cleaned by either aqueous or solvent methods.

Liquid (no residue) Flux and its use

Eliminating the cleaning of the flux after reflow saves cleaning cost, may improve product reliability, also helps environment. Cleaning with solvent or water-based cleaning agents uses expensive equipment and is costly. As the residues left behind by no-clean fluxes are inert, and non-tacky, the possibility of corrosion or harmful dust collection at the joints will not arise with rightly selected no-clean. To qualify as a no-clean flux, the material must:

1. Leave no corrosive residues
2. Leave a non-tacky residue that does not collect dust
3. Be safe and must not degrade equipment
4. Allow penetration of probe pins for electrical testing allow visual inspection of joints
5. Provide excellent solderability

No-clean fluxes typically have solid content varying from 1 to 5% as against a solid content of about 30% for "cleaning-required" fluxes. The activators in no_clean fluxes have changed chloride_containing halides to carboxylic and dicarboxylic acids.

Soldering; **Desoldering (removing components):**

Desoldering pumps and their uses

De-soldering Pumps

Solder suckers use vacuum compressed air to quickly suck air in in very quick bursts... I

have never had any luck with these at all... as a matter of fact, They Suck! The solder on

the DC Jack pins will reach the "flow" state quickly and to be able to suck up the solder

when still at its melting point and to be able to push the button and hold it steady right

over the solder just doesn't work... If you try it and it works for you... that's great... but

even the pump ones that plug in and use a solder gun like tool that has a hollow tip... when you depress the bulb quickly it will suck the solder in while heating at the same time... this does work pretty good... but after its first few uses, I find it near impossible to suck any solder let alone even be able to heat the solder to melting point.

Desoldering braid, or Solder wick/Solder braid

Solder Wick And What To Do With It

Solder Wick, also known as Desoldering Braid, is used to remove solder from the DC Jack pins. When sing it, you will need a pair of scissors to cut the braid when it gets too full of solder. Solder wick has flux added to it to help the solder flow into its braid. There are different sizes it is sold in, going from thin to wide, measured like this: 0.060", 0.080" and so on.

It is what my personal choice is for removal of solder... You can also use a "solder sucker" which is a tube tool that is spring loaded and when the button is pressed, it will suck the solder from the board. I do not use one of these and I do not recommend you do either...

Using Flux for easier removal or components or parts that are soldered onto the motherboard

The best choice to use is the flux paste, using a toothpick for the applicator. It is easier to see the paste when applied so you know exactly how much you are applying. With the liquid, it will instantly spread and is not a good choice for soldering iron use. The liquid is better for the hot air or infrared heating methods. When using the flux paste, you will apply at room temperature.

The Desoldering Process

THE DESOLDERING PROCESS

Make sure you have all your supply/tools by your work... You'll need the de-soldering braid, Your tinner, Your Solder, A Pair of Scissors, Flux Paste, A Tooth Brush, Paper Towel, Denatured Alcohol or Electrical grade circuit board cleaner (available at Radio Shack or Electronics Outlet Store), Pliers And Your Solder Sucker If You Chose To Use One...

Now, the Best way to DE solder is to start out By Capping all the Contact Pads Off with Fresh Solder... So Heat up your Soldering Iron, and Take your flux paste and dab a tiny amount of flux paste onto each dc jack contact pad from the underside of the board (the side of the Pin Ends not the side where the actual dc jack sits on...), then add a small bead of solder to the soldering iron tip and apply to the contact pad, hold there until it liquefies then quickly remove the tip ...Do this to all the Jacks pin ends...then you are Now ready to Desolder...

Continue around to the other contact pads removing the solder... it is ok if there is a small amount still stuck in the pin area, once all the pins are done, You Will Want to Clean the Motherboard... Use the Circuit board cleaner or alcohol, wipe the board and lightly go over the area with a soft bristled toothbrush...then dry by wiping the area gently with a dry paper towel or Q-tip... Be Careful doing this because there are Ceramic Capacitors on the Board near the dc jack that might rip off if you are not cautious...

Now Flip the Motherboard over to the side where the DC Jack sits... You will start with the Side Pins... the DC Jack Negative Pins on each side of the jack... Same Method Applies as the Underside, No Pre-soldering though... You will take your De-soldering Braid and lay it on top of the Solder and contact pad area, then press on the braid end with the soldering irons tip. This will remove the solder from the other side of the Jacks Pins and will clear out the C-Ring area, (the hole(s) in the board, Next do the Rear Pin(s) the same way.

Then Flip the motherboard Back Over to the Pin End Side...Add A Tiny Amount Of Flux Paste to each contact pad area once again... go over the pads quickly to remove any remaining solder, then Without using the braid, just take the soldering irons tip and go gently around the contact pad to burn away the Flux and Give the Pad A Fresh Topping..

Re-clean the Area and you can now Take the Pliers and grab ahold of the DC Jack and Gently Remove the DC Jack from the motherboard

Soldering;   **How to Solder (soldering components):**

Tinning the Tip, Repointing Your Soldering Gun Tips

Repointing or Sharpening the tip can only be done so many times, The tip is made up of layers as you can see here... And when too much of the tip is scraped away, the tip will be too soft and not be able to properly hold or flow the solder, then it's time to change the tip or throw the wand/gun out...

What I like to do is take a pair of dull scissors and scrape the tip, you can reshape the tip when doing this and get it back to however sharp of a point that you need. Then I roll the tip quickly through the inner... then get my solder on the tip.

Adding solder before removing the solder, here's why...

You are to add a small amount of fresh solder (and flux), fluxing the area first, then adding solder to the solder gun tip, then applying a small amount onto the pin/pad in need of desoldering or repair. Let cool and re-flux the area. You can now use your desoldering braid to remove the solder and you will find that you can remove more when this is done lessening the chances of contact pad damage or planer ring damage.

Holding the tip to the contact point to create "flow"

When soldering any component, the best way to get a permanent "factory quality" finish is to slightly touch the component and hold in that position until the solder has a chance to reach melting point on the component end (it already has on the solder gun tip). Then pull away the tip quickly and immediately after pulling the soldering gun tip away you will see the texture change occur to the soldered part. It will be dull or brushed looking the next second or two after the tip is taken away, then it will cool and instantly the solder texture will become shiny. When you can visually see this chemical change occurring, you will know you have done a good soldering job on that part, and it should look it.

Soldering a new trace contact pad or planer ring

You will find trace contact pads all over the laptops motherboard. If it doesn't use a pin connection then it will use a contact pad. These pads will be all different sizes and nearly all of them are rectangular in size. The pad is the end of a motherboard trace. Traces are placed all over the motherboard and they link the components, they are also located within layers of the board itself which allows them to "cross" without interference. Good thing to remember here is: whenever you remove a component from the motherboard, you must be extremely careful to not remove all of the solder from that components contact pad. Try to leave a small amount if not all because it will keep the actual contact pad below it in tact preventing damage to it.

MOTHERBOARD REPAIR

Picture Of Motherboard Showing it "split" view.. Cut in half to show the Repair of a Plated Hole.. Such as Where a DC Jack Pin Goes Through.

CONDUCTIVE COPPER FOIL TAPE

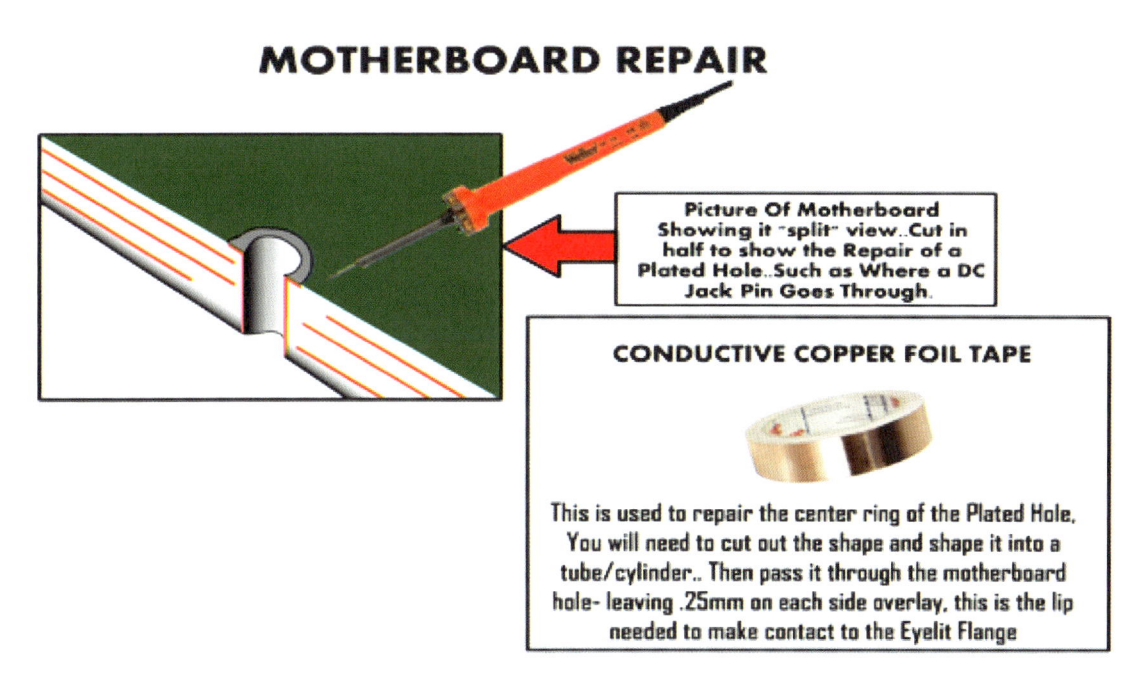

This is used to repair the center ring of the Plated Hole. You will need to cut out the shape and shape it into a tube/cylinder.. Then pass it through the motherboard hole- leaving .25mm on each side overlay, this is the lip needed to make contact to the Eyelit Flange

Traces are thin wires placed in certain patterns and configurations on the motherboard; they are molded and stamped into the board during manufacturing of the board. Some on the board will never touch the outside of the board, and some will have an access pad applied to it in manufacturing to allow a component to be added if that schematic requires it, or left dormant for possible future upgrading and additions. Then the second process of the manufacturing will stamp holes into the board that come into contact with certain traces built all throughout the motherboard. Each trace will carry a different variance of Power/data through it, and when the hole is placed in the board it will link it to the pin or pad that is attached. Then the pads are added to the motherboard, they are placed onto the planer holes made during manufacturing, they are placed on the trace ends that protruded the motherboard face during manufacturing, they are placed on pin contact points all over the board. Then to actually connect that added pad to the trace, it will need to be soldered to the trace. This is all done during the manufacturing using Machines… But it is achievable by hand as well…

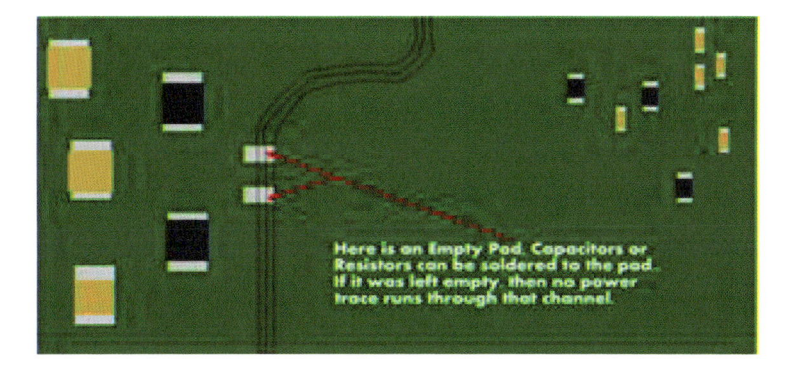

Here is an Empty Pad. Capacitors or Resistors can be soldered to the pad.. If it was left empty, then no power trace runs through that channel.

They sell ink style pens that contain liquid silver, nickel or copper to allow you to draw or paint a new trace onto the board. The same style pen is available for painting solder, and another one for painting green overcoat/insulation onto the board. You will also need to purchase copper foil tape with single sided adhesive on it. You will find this on sale at EBay and you can purchase small amounts which is all that is needed at a time. You will need to use a razor knife to cut out small rectangle shapes. You must also be using a magnifying glass for this repair. It will help you to cut out small rectangles and will allow you to see the repair area. I recommend going onto EBay or similar and buying the Head-Set style , it wraps around your head like a surgeons head-set... then it has pull up-down magnifying lenses, mine has 3 lenses that are all movable, then it has a fourth circular lens that folds up and down for 5x more zoom. It has 3 led lights on it that are adjustable up and down and left to right. This makes it totally hands free and allows you to make the repair on these traces, contact pads and c-rings.

So if you have damage to a pad, or one has ripped off or burned off, you will need to first clean the surrounding area. Use the razor blade to carefully scrape the overcoat layer around the pad location. Brush off and wipe away any particles, you want a level flat surface, do not dig down, you are to be lightly scraping, take your time. Now you need to locate the trace contact wire that connects to the pad you are repairing. Do this zooming in and light the area, you should hopefully be able to visually see the trace. If you do not see the trace, you will scrape around the contact pad location to locate it. Scrape a little deeper if you do not locate it, it will be copper in appearance and will be fragile, some traces are similar to foil tape, typically grounding traces...

But if you look closely and scrape in the right area, you will locate the trace. Once you have located the trace, you will need to scrape away any overcoat around it to reveal .5mm of it. This is where you will take and place your solder gun and apply tin to the tip, purchase a tin of tinner, dip the soldering gun tip into the tin and twirl the tip around, pull the tip out and there will be a layer of tin on your soldering gun/wand. Apply this to the contact pad repair area to be the bottom layer.

CIRCUIT FRAMES

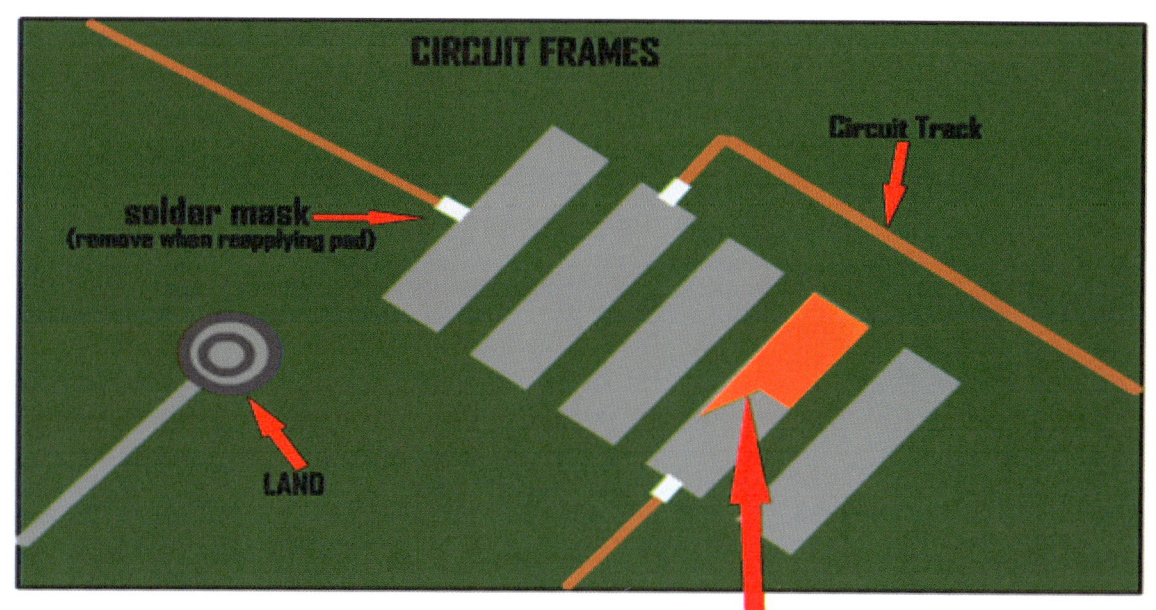

- Circuit Track
- solder mask (remove when reapplying pad)
- LAND

Damaged Pad. You will need to carefully scrape off any remaining Epoxy or Solder, then clean the area. You must also Remove the Solder From the Solder Mask, because the new pad will need to make contact with this...

Now place your copper foil tape cut out on the repair area where the pad used to be, it should adhere right in position. It should be touching the revealed trace end that you have. Now re-tin the tip and go over the copper pad and the trace to connect them, then scrape off the tip and add a small amount of solder to the tip, you want a small teardrop to be at the very end of the tip of the soldering gun/wand.

CIRCUIT TRACK REPAIR

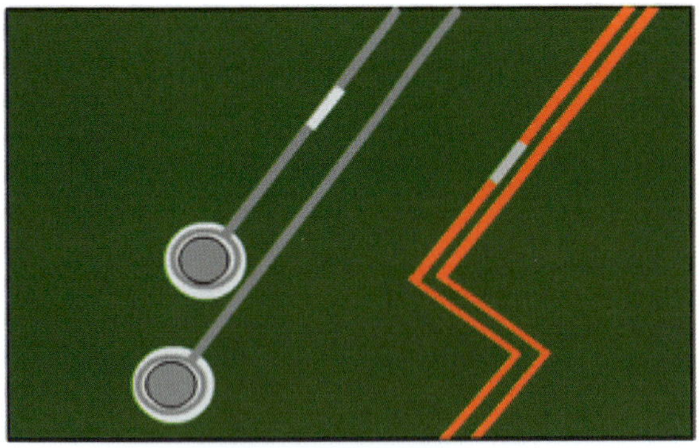

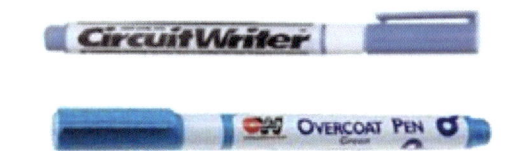

The 2 Pens Above will Repair Circuit Boards (PCBs)

The Circuit Writer, Pad, Conductive Trace, Silver Pen Will Fix Board Scratches, Pits, Burns And More...

Step 3 — Repaired Trace After Using The Green Overcoat Pen to Draw Over the Silver Trace Repair

Step 2 — A Repaired Trace

Step 1

LAND REPAIR

These Copper Donut Adhesive Pads Will Repair A Damaged Land, Or can Be Used For The DC Jack Area To ReCreate The Ring to adhere solder to.

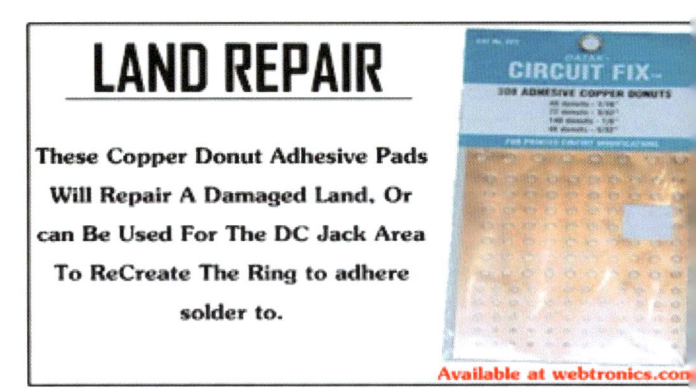

Available at webtronics.com

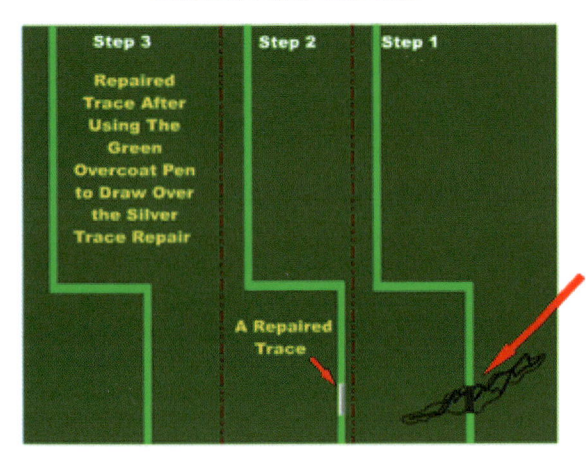

You will First Clean and Scrape the area to Prep for the New Trace. Use alcohol pad to wipe the board after gently scraping the area with your Razor blade knife. You want to carefully scrape the epoxy off of the trace on both sides of the missing area to be able to reconnect both sides using your Conductive Silver Trace Pen.

Apply this solder over the entire pad and the trace to finish the connection and complete the repair. You will now be able to reapply the missing component that was attached to the pad. This same method will apply for Pin Hole contact pads, they will be repairing the hole and the same scraping method is used ant the same trace reapplying process will be followed. You will just be wrapping the foil tape about .5mm from the holes edge or lip... and bending it into the hole area rebuilding the center ring that passes through the hole to connect all the layers throughout the board.

The Soldering Process

SOLDERING HOW TO... LEARN THE CORRECT WAY TO SOLDER MICRO COMPONENTS

Starting out, you first need to plug in the soldering iron... I recommend a 35watt or greater...

Once hot (about 2 minutes), you can begin soldering, this is assuming you have already read and followed the De-soldering process.

Start off by adding flux paste to each contact pad (both sides of the board), and to the dc jack pins. Then unravel about 6 inches worth of solder from the roll so that you can easily add more to the tip without having to take the time to unravel more each time... Lightly Scrape the Solder Gun Tip (unless new) with the scissors to give you a "fresh" tip, then quickly spin the tip in the Tinning tin...

The Gateway Ma3 and Ma7 Series have a Bad Motherboard Design Along with A Poorly designed Shell... The DC Jack sits on a little Extension board instead of placing it on the Sturdier Side of the motherboard, and over time , the plugging in and unplugging will weaken the DC Jacks connection pins due to the pins rocking back and forth from the pressure of being plugged in and not being properly braced in by the lower case.

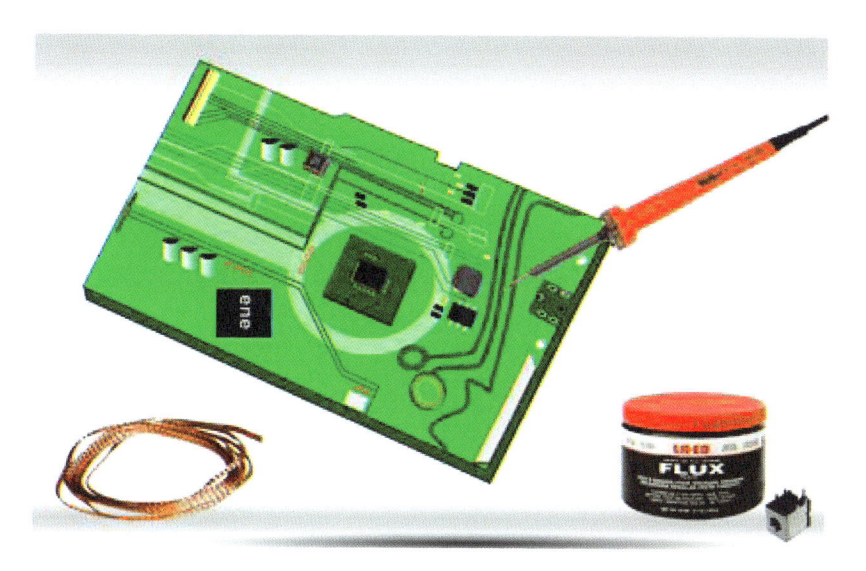

Now, back to the soldering... OK you have Fluxed everything, Your Solder Gun Is hot and ready... You Now, Place your NEW (never reuse a DC Jack... they are cheap to buy) DC Jack into position on the Motherboard, then flip the motherboard over holding the jack in place. You might need to place a few coins under the New Jack to make sure it stays Level and fits tight to the board. You are now ready to add new solder to the New DC Jack Contact Pads. Take your Soldering gun, touch the tip to the solder and get a good sized Bead onto the tip... Make sure you hold the soldering iron with the tip pointing downward... this way the solder won't flow up the tip and it will stay at the point.

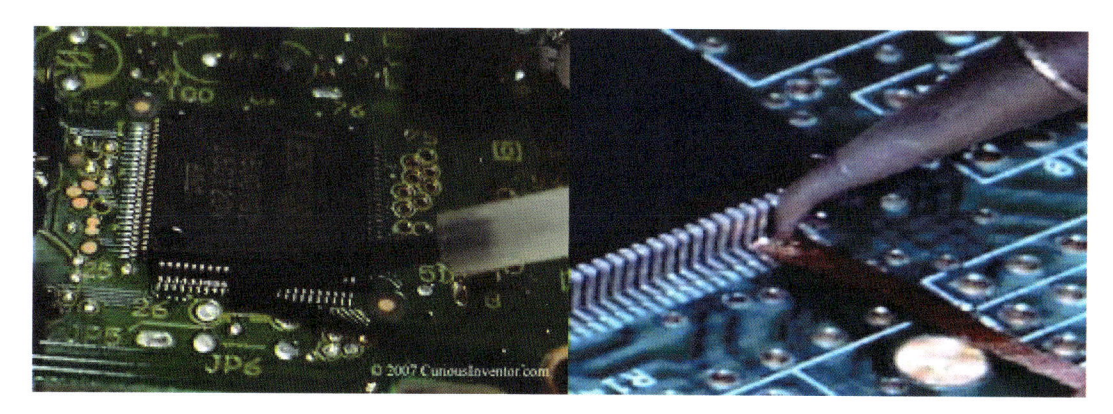

Now, bring the soldering iron tip to the contact pad, starting out doing only 1 pin at a time... I usually start with the Side Pins (the Negative Pins) and then doing the Back Pin(s) which is/are the positive pins. Once you touch the solder guns tip to the pad, you want to see it suck into the hole... you will see it sink down and then it will evenly flow around the Pin to cover the whole contact pad... at this point, You can pull the solder iron tip away from the motherboard and the Solder will instantly harden... If you can visibly see that the solder did not cover the entire pad, then go back and add a little more solder but no more flux...

Continue To the next pin/pad until complete, you should have Smooth Bumps, Not rigid sharp pointy caps...If you do, you didn't use enough Flux. Make Sure you repair the C-Rings on any Contact Pad that is missing one... And if the contact pad itself ripped off, you will have to carefully scrape the area using a utility knife to scrape away the green coating and get to the copper sheet layer, then Tin your solder iron real good and run the tip of the soldering gun around the exposed copper where the contact pad used to be...

Software Issues and Repair How-To

Software Issues and Repair How-To; **Blue Screen Issues:**

Blue screen issues

Blue screen issues can happen due to many reasons. And yes, there are codes in the error screen that can help you pinpoint the specific error at hand, a lot of the times, the error given is a "generalized" error and has no one specific meaning to one specific hardware or software failure issue. A good thing to look for when blue screens occur is Taking Note as to when they occur. Noting when they occur will greatly help you in determining the issue at hand.

You need to find out first of all, is the blue screen happening at the same time with every powering up? Does it happen before reaching the Desktop? Does it happen once at the desktop, and is it consistent?

Blue screens that are happening before reaching the desktop can be a few things, Use the error screen as a guide... You will typically see blue screening due to hard drive failure or a hard drive in the beginning stages of failure. Blue screening will also happen due to failing RAM, or if a faulty RAM slot, you will need to reseat Memory sticks, and if able, run a Memory diagnosis test in the BIOS Setup Utility (F2). The Boot up Process also is the time when your system drivers are loading, and if corrupted, a failing or faulty device driver can issue a blue screen. I have seen a lot of cases lately where windows updates had gone awry (a-rye), and left the Operating System Unbootable. It was concluded that the updates being Auto-Installed had set out a service Pack Update for a different Operating system version... Meaning, the laptop in question was doing an auto install on an XP based Laptop... and the Service Pack that was mistakenly added and installed was a Windows 7 Service Update that somehow had gotten added into your updates downloads. When this occurs, the system will typically "dump" the existing driver or patch, and replace it with the updated one... But if it happens to be one for a totally different version of Windows update, it will Leave a Fault in the Core files that Upon rebooting the Laptop, will leave the Operating System unable to Pass the Loading of system drivers area of the Boot process and will either Blue Screen, or will freeze the Boot Up or will cause a Reboot Continuous cycle.

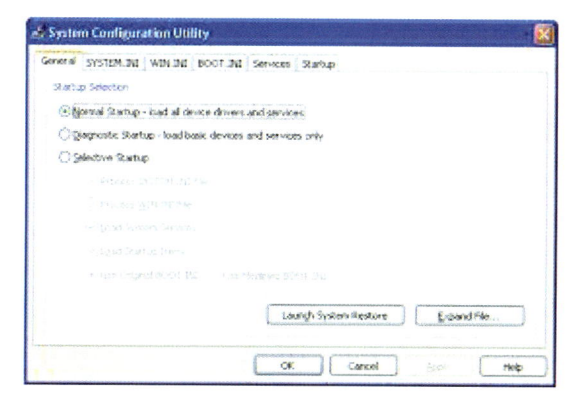

Blue Screens that occur after the laptop has booted past the Log In Screen, Yet they occur before reaching the desktop or very shortly after (like before all start up items are loaded), can usually be attributed to Software conflicts... and can rarely mean that the hard drive is beginning to fail... though in most cases it will end up being software... Software Conflicts that can cause the blue screen/non-booting issue:

More than one Antivirus Program running that conflict with one another... Or those same 2 programs running and one expires, the other one will override the expired one and the expired one will cause issues. A good example is Norton 360 installed and trend Micro Internet Security Suite Installed, Both Running Together... (both Full packages), one of the running programs detects a driver file as being corrupted, and dumps it, not allowing that driver to be reinstalled. Believe it or not, this happens to a lot of systems... People not fully understanding how Security Software works, They Go and Install 4 or 5 Different Programs ... and then enable all to run at the same time, all the time... Then The System ends up going haywire due to too many programs fighting to monitor the users every move on the laptop... Only one wins and the others either bypass the error, or they send the software program into a self-error. This end result is a Blue Screen Error, due to Non Functional Drivers, Removed system files and so on...

Blue screens that will occur when the system has fully booted to the desktop and all startup items have finished loading, can most likely be attributed to Overheating Issues, though they will happen at different times, not the same time every boot up... If it is occurring at the same time like when you attempt to go to the internet, you will have to first look at the Device Manager to see if there are any error icons next to any drivers. Next thing to do is go into your system configuration utility. To do this, Click on START on the Desktop (lower left corner), then in the Text Search Box (in XP you click on RUN) you type: msconfig, press enter key, now your sys config utility window will pop up... Note here that a mini pop up might appear before the sys config window, it is only asking permission to open sys config... so agree...

Now that you have the Sys Configuration Window open... you will see Tabs, you will first click on the Start Up tab. In the Start Up tab, you will first glance through the list, now click on Disable All from the choices. Note here that initially you will Disable All for testing purposes and to see if conflicts disappear upon reboot, you can always go back into this list to re-enable any antivirus or Wi-Fi software you may want or need to be running...

Next Click Apply from the choices, you are now going to select the Services Tab (right next to Start Up Tab). In the Services tab, you will see below the list: Hide All Microsoft Services... You will put a check mark in that box to hide them... Then The List above will shorten... You will now choose: Disable All from the choices, and click Apply, then click OK... The next pop up window will tell you to Reboot, which you do. Note here that some laptops will throw up an Administrator warning... Just Agree and close that window... then Reboot.

Upon Reboot... You are to be checking if the Blue Screening Stops.

OPERATING SYSTEM NOT INSTALLING

OPERATING SYSTEM NOT INSTALLING; SATA DRIVE NOT RECOGNISED ISSUE:

Configuring the BIOS

Close your computer case and restart your computer. Your computer may automatically detect your new drive. If your computer does not automatically detect your new drive, follow the steps below.

1. Restart your computer. While the computer restarts, run the system setup program (sometimes called BIOS or CMOS setup). This is usually done by pressing a special key, such as DELETE, ESC, or F1 during the startup process.

2. Within the system setup program, instruct the system to auto detect your new drive.

3. Save the settings and exit the setup program. When your computer restarts, it should recognize your new drive. If your system still doesn't recognize your new drive, see the troubleshooting section on the back of this sheet.

Note: Serial ATA is a new interface type. Some older systems may see the drive and classify it as a SCSI device if you are using a Serial ATA host adapter. This is normal even though this is not a SCSI disc drive. Many systems' BIOS will not identify a Serial ATA drive connected to a PCI SATA host adapter. This is because a PCI SATA Host Adapter has its own BIOS which is used to identify hard drives connected to it which is separate from the BIOS of the computer. To determine whether or not the SATA Host Adapter is detecting the Serial ATA hard drive, please consult the documentation provided by the Serial ATA Host Adapter's manufacturer. This does not affect drive performance or capacity.

APPLE BOOT KEY COMBINATIONS

Apple Boot Key Combos:

Bypass startup drive and boot from external (or CD).... CMD-OPT-SHIFT-DELETE

Boot from CD (Most late model Apples) C

Force the internal hard drive to be the boot drive .... D

Boot from a specific SCSI ID #.(#=SCSI ID number)...... CMD-OPT-SHIFT-DELETE-#

Zap PRAM .... CMD-OPT-P-R

Boot into open Firmware .... CMD-OPT-O-F

Clear NV RAM. Similar to reset-all in open Firmware ... CMD-OPT-N-V

Disable Extensions .... SHIFT

Rebuild Desktop .... CMD-OPT

Close finder windows.(hold just before finder starts).. OPT

Boot with Virtual Memory off............................ CMD

Trigger extension manager at boot-up.................... SPACE

Force Quadra av machines to use TV as a monitor........ CMD-OPT-T-V

Boot from ROM (Mac Classic only)....................... CMD-OPT-X-O

Force PowerBooks to reset the screen................... R

Force an AV monitor to be recognized as one............ CMD-OPT-A-V

Eject Boot Floppy....................................... Hold Down Mouse Button Select volume to start from............................ OPT

Start in Fire wire target drive mode.................... T

Startup in OSX if OS9 and OXS in boot partition........ X or CMD-X

Attempt to boot from network server .... N   (Hold until Mac Logo appears)Hold down until the 2nd chime, will boot into 9?....... CMD-OPT

OSX: Watch the status of the system load............... CMD-V

OSX: Enter single-user mode (shell-level mode)......... CMD-S

After startup:

Bring up dialogue for shutdown/sleep/restart........... POWER

Eject a Floppy Disk.................................... CMD-SHIFT-1 or(2) or (0)

Force current app to quit.............................. CMD-OPT-ESC

Unconditionally reboot................................. CTRL-CMD-POWER

Fast Shutdown………………………………… CTRL-CMD-OPT-POWER

Go to the debugger (if MacsBug is installed)………… CMD-POWER

Put late model PowerBooks & Desktops to sleep……….. CMD-OPT-POWER

Application Specific Keys:

Startup key combos to reset the resolution on video boards: SuperMac (at least some models)press & hold………….. OPT

Imagine 128 Card (reset resolution)………………… N

RasterOps (at least some models)press & hold…………. CMD-OPT-SHIFT

Radius (Use cable sense pins to set resolution)…….. U

Radius (Cycle through available resolutions)……….. T

Conflict Catcher: Pause Boot………………………………. P

Launch CC at Startup……………………… SPACE or CAPS LOCK

Skip remaining extensions………………………. CMD-PERIOD

Reboot cleanly while loading extensions………….. CMD-R

RAM Doubler/Disable at Startup………………………….. ~ (Tilde) or ESC

Apple System Installer: Change custom install to clean install……………. CMD-Shift-K

Claris Emailer:Bypass specified startup connections……………… Hold CMD at launch; Bring up rebuild options………………………. Hold OPT at launch

---

Controlling the Post-Startup Environment

Most Macintosh users know about holding the Shift key down to prevent extensions from loading, but there are numerous startup modifiers that affect the state of the system after the boot process finishes.

* Shift causes the Mac to boot without extensions, which is useful for troubleshooting extension conflicts. If you hold down Shift after all the extensions have loaded but before the Finder launches, it also prevents any startup items from launching.

* Spacebar launches Apple's Extensions Manager early in the startup process so you can enable or disable extensions before they load. Casady & Greene's Conflict Catcher, if you're using it instead of Extensions Manager, also launches if it sees you holding down the spacebar, or, optionally, if Caps Lock is activated. Conflict Catcher also adds the capability to configure additional startup keys as ways of specifying that a particular startup set should be used. Choose Edit Sets from the Sets menu, select a set in the resulting dialog and click Modify. In the sub-dialog that appears, you can specify a startup key and check the checkbox to make it effective.

* Option, if held down as the Finder launches, closes any previously open Finder windows. On stock older Macs, holding down Option does nothing at startup by default, although some extensions may deactivate if Option is held down when they attempt to load; see below for Option's effect on new Macs and Macs with Zip drives.

* Control can cause the Location Manager to prompt you to select a location. Although Control is the default, you can redefine it in the Location Manager's Preferences dialog, and since Control held down at startup also activates Apple's MacsBug debugger (see below), you may wish to pick a different key combination.

* Command turns virtual memory off until the next restart.

* Shift-Option disables extensions other than Connectix's RAM Doubler (and MacsBug - see below). To disable RAM Doubler but no other extensions, hold down the tilde (~) key at startup.

Choosing Startup Disks

Not surprisingly, many of the startup modifiers affect the disk used to boot the Mac. A number of these are specific to certain models of the Macintosh.

* The mouse button causes the Mac to eject floppy disks and most other forms of removable media, though not CD-ROMs.

* The C key forces the Mac to start up from a bootable CD-ROM, if one is present, which is useful if something goes wrong with your startup hard disk. This key doesn't work with some older Macs or clones that didn't use Apple CD-ROM drives; they require Command- Shift-Option-Delete instead (see below).

* Option activates the new Startup Manager on the iBook, Power Mac G4 (AGP Graphics), PowerBook (FireWire), and slot-loading iMacs. The Startup Manager displays a rather cryptic set of icons indicating available startup volumes, including any NetBoot volumes that are available. On some Macs with Iomega Zip drives, holding down Option at startup when there is a Zip startup disk inserted will cause the Mac to boot from the Zip disk.

* Command-Shift-Option-Delete bypasses the disk selected in the Startup Disk control panel in favor of an external device or from CD-ROM (on older Macs). This is also useful if your main hard disk is having problems and you need to start up from another device. (On some PowerBooks, however, this key combination merely ignores the internal drive, which isn't as useful.)

* The D key forces the PowerBook (Bronze Keyboard and FireWire) to boot from the internal hard disk.

* The T key forces the PowerBook (FireWire) (and reportedly the Power Mac G4 (AGP Graphics), though I was unable to verify that on my machine) to start up in FireWire Target Disk Mode, which is essentially the modern equivalent of SCSI Disk Mode and enables a PowerBook (FireWire) to act as a FireWire-accessible hard disk for another Macintosh.

Seriously Tweaky Startup Modifiers

Only programmers and the most geeky of users will find these startup modifiers useful.

* Control activates Apple's MacsBug debugger as soon as it loads. If you rely on this frequently, you may want to redefine the default key for selecting the Location Manager location at startup from Control to something else.

* Shift-Option disables extensions and virtual memory but still loads MacsBug, which would otherwise be disabled by the Shift key.

* Command-Option-O-F puts you into Open Firmware mode on PCI-based Macs and clones. Open Firmware is a cross-platform firmware standard for controlling hardware that all PCI-based Macs use. It's mostly of interest to hardware developers, but it can be a fun way to freak out a new user who's not expecting to see a command line on the Mac. To exit Open Firmware and continue booting, type "mac-boot" or "bye" (depending on Macintosh model) and press Return. For a list of commands you can enter while in Open Firmware mode, see the Tech Info Library article.

Just for Fun

Although Apple has moved away from relatively frivolous "Easter Eggs" connected with startup modifiers, there are a few available for old Macintosh models.

* Command-X-O, when held down at startup on a Macintosh Classic boots the Classic from a built-in ROM disk.

* Command-Option-C-I, when held down at startup on a Macintosh IIci whose date has been set to 20-Sep-89 (the machine's introduction date), produces some sort of graphical display that I can't check for lack of a relevant machine. A different display appears if you hold down Command-Option-F-X at startup on a Macintosh IIfx with the date set to 19-Mar-90.

Printed in Great Britain
by Amazon